a short & happy guide to

Acing Your 1L Year

Adam M. Gershowitz
James D. & Pamela J. Penny Research Professor
William & Mary Law School

A SHORT & HAPPY GUIDE® SERIES

WEST ACADEMIC

860 Blue Gentian Road, Suite 350
Eagan, MN 55121
1-877-888-1330

Published in the United States of America

ISBN: 979-8-89209-874-8

Acknowledgments

This book was fun to write. I had terrific 1L teachers when I was a law student and, as a result, much of the 1L material has stuck with me for years. But, let's be honest, when more than two decades go by you definitely forget some things.

For a criminal law professor to write a book about the entire 1L experience I had to do some studying. Even then, I needed some extra help from professors who teach the 1L courses every year. I am very grateful to my wonderful colleagues at William & Mary who have helped me along the way. In particular, I want to thank Aaron Bruhl, Laura Heymann, Eric Kades, Laura Killinger, Alli Larsen, Tom McSweeney, Sarah Rajec, and James Stern who read chapters or answered questions. Thanks also to my research assistant, Ryan Zimmerman, for providing a recent 1L's perspective on the entire book.

Finally, I want to express my gratitude to my college mentor, Professor Ken Haas, for guiding me to law school. If this book had been around back then, he definitely would have made me read it!

Table of Contents

A Short & Happy Guide to Acing Your 1L Year

CHAPTER 1

Welcome to Law School—an Introduction to What You Need to Know

Welcome! If you've opened this book you are on your way to law school or at least thinking seriously about it. You are probably curious, excited, and . . . a little scared. But don't worry. This book will explain everything you need to know to ace your first year of law school.

1. The Great Parts About Law School

Let's start with the exciting part. You are going to learn a ton of useful information in law school. Law school is going to turn you into the person who actually knows the answer to the question "Is that even legal?" When your friends or family get into trouble or have questions, you'll be able to answer them or at least point them in the right direction. That's a pretty cool skill.

But learning the rules is just the beginning. After all, you wouldn't pay three years of tuition just to memorize some rules you could find in the library. Lawyers are valuable not only because they know a lot of law, but also because they can use logic to figure out the right answer when it isn't written in a book.

Law school will push you to "think like a lawyer." Your professors will train you how to pick apart a problem and critically analyze it. You will learn to see fine gradations between different cases. And you will learn how to take a rule from one case and determine whether it can be applied in a different scenario. If you've gotten into law school, you are already smart. Law school will take your analytical skills and put them on steroids.

An added bonus of law school besides learning lots of rules and critical thinking is that you will make lifelong friends. As you take your classes, you will be surrounded by other smart and interesting people. And you will form a close bond with your classmates. Some of your 1L friends will end up as your roommates, law firm partners, and best friends. If you're lucky like me, you may even meet your spouse in law school!

2. The Challenging Parts About Law School

Law school can be a terrific professional and personal experience, but it can also be very challenging as well. There are a couple of reasons.

First, your 1L year will be like drinking from a firehose. You will spend a lot of time in class, and you will have to do a lot of reading. And most of the subject matter will be entirely new to you. While you may know a little about Criminal Law, odds are that you will be swimming in new waters when it comes to Civil Procedure, Contracts, Torts, Property, Constitutional Law, and Legal Research and Writing.

So a lot of the material you read in law school will be entirely new to you. To make matters more challenging, some of what you read will not be easy to understand. Legal doctrine is based on precedent dating back hundreds of years. You will read some judicial decisions that will seem like they were written by aliens who never set foot on Planet Earth. In some ways, law is like learning a foreign language.

Second, the classroom experience will be harder and more intimidating than your undergraduate courses. In college, you probably spent most of your class time listening to your professors give lectures. Your professors did most of the work. In law school, the professors turn the tables and make the students do more of the heavy lifting. Law professors typically use the Socratic Method. Professors will call on you out of the blue and quiz you in great detail about the cases you read as well as hypotheticals you have never thought about. Professors will carry on a conversation with you in which they use your answers to elicit the legal rules and show the class the correct analysis. Many law school professors never come out and say what the right answer is. They think that amounts to "spoon-feeding." Law professors think anyone can look something up in a book or write down what an instructor tells them. Law professors want you to learn how to figure out the answers yourself because that's what lawyers do in practice every day. The Socratic Method can be intimidating.

Third, you will study differently in law school because law school exams are very different from the tests you took in college. As an undergraduate student, you probably read (or skimmed) the assigned reading, took notes in class, re-read those notes before the exam, and then repeated back the information on the test. If you remembered what the professor told you, then you earned a good grade.

Law school exams are harder. The professor almost never asks you to regurgitate the details of what you read. Instead, the professor wants you to take the principles from the cases you read and apply them to entirely different factual situations. In short, you need to extract the principles and rules from the cases and then figure out how those rules should apply when the facts are changed. This is not an easy task.

Fourth and finally, law school requires you to write more clearly than you have before. Legal writing is a unique skill and it is crucial for performing well on your exams. For most law school exams, the professor invents a fake (and lengthy) factual scenario. And the professor doesn't usually tell you what specific things to write about. Instead, she expects you to figure out what the key issues are, and she expects you to clearly explain how the legal questions should be resolved. Doing this requires not just that you know the rules, but that you can explain them in a clear, organized fashion. Just because you studied all semester doesn't mean the professor can tell that you understand the material. You have to be able to communicate what you have learned in a clear, succinct, logical way. And that is also not easy to do.

3. What This Book Will Do for You and Why You Should Read It

The four challenges I listed above can be intimidating. I know because I was once a frightened 1L. When I started law school, I had never met a lawyer. When I walked in my Torts class on the first day, I didn't know what the word "torts" meant. No one ever gave me a heads up about the Socratic Method. I had no idea how I was supposed to be preparing for my exams. Like thousands of 1Ls who came before me, my mind was spinning and I sometimes felt overwhelmed.

If you are like me, you might be thinking, "Am I cut out for this? Can I really do this?" The answer is "Yes, you can do this, and this book can help you." I wrote this book to make law school less intimidating and to help give you a head start. Here's what I will show you in the pages that follow.

First, this book will go through your 1L courses one at a time and show you the most important topics you will cover in each course. I will show you the foundational legal doctrines for each course so that you have a general overview of each course *before* you start to dig into the details. My goal is obviously not to teach you everything you need to know for every one of your classes. That would be impossible.

The point of this book is to make sure you don't "miss the forest for the trees." That expression means that you shouldn't get so bogged down in the details of a topic that you miss the big picture. One of the biggest problems law students encounter—especially in their 1L year—is that they get lost in the morass of all the legal rules they are learning. Your classes will be filled with rules, exceptions to rules, and exceptions to those exceptions. Before you know it, you will be staring really closely at the trees.

Now don't get me wrong, the trees are important. Your professor is going to test you on the legal doctrine she taught in class. But law school is not only about memorizing the rules. It is about understanding *why* the court adopted those rules and *how* the rules fit together to show the entire puzzle. You need to understand what the legal doctrine is doing in order to apply it to the next case. If you only focus on the rules, you will miss the big picture.

The problem is that it is hard to see the big picture while you are also learning lots of detailed rules. You've probably heard the expression that it is hard to fly an airplane while building it. That means it's hard to do something while you are still learning *what* you should be doing. To deal with that challenge, I want you to have a very basic understanding of what each of your 1L subjects is about *before* you walk into your first class. This book aims to show you the big picture up front, before you have to dig into all the details. So the first thing this book does is give you a preview—one short chapter at a time—of each of your 1L classes.

The second thing this book does is show you how to prepare for the Socratic Method that your professor will use in class. As I'll explain, you can't just read the assigned pages and show up for class. Instead, you will have to write a brief that summarizes the facts and legal analysis of the cases that you read. The brief forces you to analyze the cases and be sure you understand them. And the brief becomes a great tool for you to use if the professor calls on you in class. I'll show you step-by-step how to brief cases so that you'll be prepared when your professor calls on you.

The third thing this book does is show you how to prepare for your exams. Law school exams are usually lengthy essay questions that ask you to apply the rules you learned during the semester. How do you prepare for a law school exam? You have to write an outline of the course that sets out all the key rules you learned during the semester and how they fit together. To do this, you have to strip away the irrelevant facts from the cases you read and reduce the cases to very specific rules. I will show you step-by-step how to write an effective outline.

I will also walk you through which study guides you might want to buy and which ones you shouldn't waste your time and money on. I'll talk to you about forming study groups, and I'll explain when they are a good use of your time and when they're not. And most importantly, I will show you how to take practice exams in a way that actually improves your exam-taking skills rather than just scaring you.

The fourth thing this book will do is show you how to write a great exam answer. Remember, law school is not like college. You will not be tested primarily on memorization. Instead, law professors want to see that you can spot the major issues and apply the legal principles you've learned to new situations. And you have to write your answers in a clear, organized way. There is an art to taking law school exams. All the studying in the world does you no good unless you can convey to the professor what you have learned.

After grading thousands of exams, I can tell you that there are very clear differences between a good exam answer and a bad exam answer. Professors understand these differences, but 1L students almost never do. Most law students go into their first exams totally cold, with no understanding of what the professor is looking for. I am going to give away the secret and walk you through how to write a great exam answer.

4. Our Plan of Action

So, here's the plan. The beginning of this book includes a chapter for each of the major subjects in the 1L year—Criminal Law, Torts, Civil Procedure, Contracts, Constitutional Law, Property, and Legal Research and Writing. These chapters will explain the big picture issues you will cover in each class and the most important legal principles.

As you read the chapters about each of the 1L subjects, don't feel the need to take notes or use a highlighter. Remember that the goal is just to get a basic understanding of the topics your professor is going to cover and how they fit together. You don't have to memorize any of the rules now. Your goal is just to let a picture of the forest sink in before you start focusing on all the trees.

After covering the substance of each 1L course, I explain the strategies you'll need to ace each of those courses. I spell out how to prepare for class, how to organize your notes after class, which study guides to buy and not buy, how to outline, how to take practice tests, and how to write a great exam answer.

All else being equal, I suggest reading the book in order. (Before you can learn how to prepare for classes and exams, it helps to understand what subjects you'll be studying.) But you do you. If you would rather bounce around from chapter to chapter, that's totally fine. The key point is that you should use this book as a resource to get a feel for the 1L year and how to succeed in the courses you'll be taking.

Let's get started!

CHAPTER 2

Criminal Law

After years of watching television and movies, you might think you know what 1L Criminal Law will be about. But you're probably mistaken. If you are expecting to learn about police officers interrogating people or searching their cars, then you are a little ahead of the game. The law of search and seizure and interrogations is definitely covered in law school, but not until you take Criminal *Procedure* as a 2L or 3L. Nor will your 1L Criminal Law class be about making objections to witness testimony or learning how to give a closing argument. Those classes—Evidence and Trial Advocacy—are also upper-level courses that you will take later.

1. Learning About a Small Number of Crimes in a Lot of Detail

The 1L Criminal Law course is primarily about understanding a small number of crimes in a lot of detail. Each instructor makes their own syllabus, but the odds are that your 1L Criminal Law course will focus on murder, manslaughter, sexual assault, robbery, burglary, and larceny. And after you've figured out those crimes, your professor will almost certainly spend time on the crime of attempt (where you try but fail to commit a crime), accomplice liability (a theory where you are guilty for helping someone else to commit a crime), and conspiracy (the crime of agreeing with another person to commit a crime, even if you never manage to pull it off). The 1L Criminal Law course is often called *substantive* criminal law, because you will be learning the substantive elements of these crimes.

Why will you spend so much time on a handful of crimes? It is certainly not because those are the most common crimes in the United States. More than a million people are arrested for drunk driving in the United States each year, compared to 20,000 murders. Yet, you will probably spend multiple classes on murder, but none on drunk driving. Nor do professors focus on murder and conspiracy because they are the only interesting crimes. There are lots of other fascinating crimes. You probably didn't know that Texas's criminal code specifically makes it a crime to assemble an amusement park ride while intoxicated. And you probably weren't aware that the federal government makes it a crime for a merchant to rip the tags off of a mattress.

Criminal law professors focus on a handful of crimes because they are using these crimes to teach you big-picture concepts that you will use to analyze every other crime that is on the books. In other words, when a professor spends a long time teaching you the elements of murder, they definitely want you to understand the legal principles for murder. But perhaps more importantly, they want you to be able to apply the concept that you have learned to other crimes. So what are the concepts that professors are trying to get across in your Criminal Law course?

2. Actus Reus and Mens Rea

First, there are some core elements that are present in almost all criminal statutes. Most crimes have a so-called actus reus and a mens rea. The actus reus is the action that the defendant takes to commit the crime. In theft cases, the actus reus is grabbing the property. In burglary cases, the actus reus is the breaking and entering. In murder cases, the actus reus is the shooting, stabbing, or punching (or some other action) the defendant does to kill the victim.

The mens rea is the defendant's mental state. We all remember the key question parents asked us when we were kids and messed something up: "Did you do it on purpose?" or "Did you do it by accident?" Criminal Law takes those basic concepts and makes them more complicated. You will see words like "intentional," "deliberate," "willful," and "malicious" to name just a few. Your professor may force you to struggle with how these concepts are different from each other and whether they can be reduced to any clear definition. (Spoiler alert: These terms are usually very hard to define and apply consistently.)

Perhaps because there are so many vague mens rea terms, modern laws have tried to simplify matters by using four mens rea concepts: (1) purposely, (2) knowingly, (3) recklessly, and (4) negligently. Not every modern criminal statute uses these four mens rea concepts, but a lot do. As a result, you will spend a lot of time trying to figure out what they mean and how to apply them to routine cases. In studying the most common mens rea terms, you will eventually see how they operate in a hierarchical fashion from most serious to least. Below is an early preview of those mens rea terms. Like Law School, I set them out here not just to teach you a little law, but also so that you can begin to appreciate how you will be approaching all kinds of other problems with precision.

(1) Purposely: A defendant hopes something will happen. For example, the defendant *wants* to kill the victim.

(2) Knowingly: A defendant is aware that something will *almost certainly* happen, even if they don't really

care whether it happens or not. Imagine that Alvin and Barry are standing right next to each other. The defendant then takes out his high-powered gun, aims it at Alvin's and says "I have no beef with Barry. I don't want Barry to die. But I do know that this is a really powerful gun." Then imagine that the defendant shoots Alvin and the bullet goes straight through Alvin and strikes Barry and kills him as well. The prosecutor can probably show that the defendant "knows" that firing the high-powered gun would kill Barry, even if it wasn't his purpose to kill him.

(3) Recklessly: A defendant is *aware* of a *substantial and unjustifiable risk* that their actions will cause some harm, but takes the action anyway. Imagine that a driver is speeding through a neighborhood at 3:00pm behind a bright yellow school bus that is dropping off children. The driver speeds around the bus while it is stopped. The driver doesn't want to run over a child (so there is no purposeful mens rea). And the driver doesn't know to a near certainty that they will kill a child by speeding around the bus (so there is no knowledge mens rea). But the driver is aware that they are doing something risky and unacceptable. So if the driver does in fact hit and kill a child, they will have done so recklessly.

(4) Negligently: A defendant is *not* aware of an unacceptable risk but they *should have been* aware of it. Imagine the same speeding driver trailing behind the school bus. Imagine though that the bus is blue instead of bright yellow and that it is 6:00pm instead of 3:00pm. (Maybe this is the after-school

activities bus that drops off students who stayed late for sports and clubs.) The defendant has been lost in thought and does not notice students get off at the first few stops. She is not aware of the risk and therefore is not reckless. But an ordinary person behaving properly in society would have been paying attention and would have understood that she was following a school bus. So our driver *should have been* aware of the risk that she engaged in by speeding around the school bus. She was therefore negligent.

To summarize, most criminal statutes require *both* an actus reus and a mens rea. The criminal law requires an actus reus because we do not normally punish people just because they wanted to do something bad. They must have actually taken an action. And the criminal law requires a mens rea because we do not normally punish people just because they did an action that caused some harm. They must have had a culpable mental state when they took that action.

Put differently, in the United States, we don't punish people because they are disagreeable, rotten people. And we don't punish people who do harmful things entirely by accident. A person can behave badly without actually committing a crime. As such, you need to look carefully at the criminal statute and check to make sure that the defendant had both the actus reus and mens rea.

3. Focusing on the Elements That Make up Criminal Statutes

In focusing on actus reus and mens rea, your Criminal Law professor will eventually move beyond the abstract big-picture concepts and will begin to focus on particular crimes. In studying particular crimes, you will carefully study the statutes written by legislatures. Right off the bat, you will notice that the legislature does not just say "murder is illegal" or that "stealing is against the law." Rather, the legislature specifically defines what murder and burglary are by listing very detailed elements that a prosecutor must prove in order to convict a defendant of those crimes. For example, a state statute might define burglary as "breaking and entering the dwelling of another at nighttime with intent to commit a felony inside."

Your criminal law professor will direct your attention to the burglary statute and will push you (1) to understand the elements in the statute, and (2) to consider whether there is evidence in the case for each one of those elements.

Consider this simple hypothetical: Your friend Carrie comes by to visit. She knocks on the front door to your house and you let her in. After the two of you talk for an hour, you go to the bathroom. While you are gone, Carrie notices (for the first time) your diamond bracelet, which is sitting on a nearby table. Carrie picks up the bracelet and puts it in her pocket. When you come back from the bathroom, Carrie talks to you for a little longer and then leaves the house, taking the diamond bracelet with her.

If you ask your pre-law school self if Carrie stole the bracelet, your answer will probably be "yes." Carrie took something that did not belong to her without permission. But that is not the question your professor will ask. Instead, the professor's question will be "Did Carrie commit a burglary?" And the answer is "no," because Carrie's actions do not meet the elements of the burglary statute. Carrie was invited into the house and therefore she never engaged in a "breaking." Plus, the hypothetical does not tell us whether Carrie took the bracelet at "nighttime" as the statute requires. Moreover, while Carrie clearly intended to take the bracelet when she placed it in her pocket, did she have that intent when she entered the house? Probably not, since the hypothetical says that Carrie noticed the bracelet "for the first time" only after already having entered the house over an hour earlier. The key point is not to ask whether Carrie did something wrongful—she surely did. Rather, the key question is whether Carrie's actions met the elements of the burglary statute.

To recap so far, your Criminal Law class will introduce you to core big-picture concepts like actus reus and mens rea. You will then move on to apply those concepts for specific offenses like murder and burglary. In analyzing those crimes, you will not be memorizing the murder and burglary statutes of 50 states or learning how much prison time someone gets for violating those statutes. Instead, you will focus on the elements of each crime and whether there are sufficient facts to demonstrate those elements.

4. What to Do When the Statute Doesn't Directly Answer the Question

The next thing your professor will do is ask you to analyze tricky situations in which the plain text of the law does not appear to tell you the answer. Life is complicated and there are a million ways that someone could take property (or kill another person, or commit some other crime). Legislatures cannot anticipate everything, so they write statues to be broad enough to cover most situations, but not so broad that the laws would be vague and unclear. In other words, statutes do not contain a laundry list of every possible situation that could occur in life. And sometimes it is unclear whether the defendant's actions fall within the definition of the crime or not.

Let's go back to our burglary statute which states that someone commits a burglary by "breaking and entering the dwelling of another at nighttime with intent to commit a felony inside." Now think about these tough questions:

1. Is "breaking" limited to smashing a window or knocking down a door? If the door is unlocked and you twist the handle to open the door (or if the window is unlocked and you push it up), is that a breaking?
2. If you reach into an open window and lift out a necklace sitting on a nearby dresser, does that amount to entering? Can it be "entering" if only my arm goes inside the window? What if I never stick my arm or hand in the window at all and instead use a tool—think of something as simple as a shovel or a rake—to scoop up the necklace and pull it out of the house?
3. Is a garage a dwelling? What about an outhouse? Or a tool shed? Could a motor home be a dwelling if it is parked on the street?
4. Is it nighttime if the sun has fallen below the horizon but there is still some daylight left?
5. Can it be a burglary if the defendant is caught inside the home and never made off with the jewels?

These questions—and dozens like them—are the bread-and-butter of a law school Criminal Law class. You will read court decisions that interpret the statutes and try to answer these questions. Courts will turn to the legislative history, public policy arguments, fairness principles, and other interpretive methods in their efforts to get to the right answer.

For instance, courts might say that the reason a burglary statute requires the crime to be at nighttime is that it is scarier to have your home broken into when it is dark and when you cannot see who is in the house and what they are doing. So if there is enough daylight left to be able to see a person's face, the court might conclude that it is not "nighttime," even if the sun has set below the horizon. Of course, that logic is debatable. Burglary is a serious crime, so maybe nighttime should be defined expansively to deter potential criminals from breaking into people's homes. On the other hand, because burglary is a serious crime that carries serious prison time, maybe we should be reluctant to interpret it in a way that makes it easier for the prosecution to convict people.

Around and around you will go as you wrestle with questions as simple as "what does nighttime mean?" Sometimes there will be a right answer; sometimes there will be a "better" answer; and sometimes there will be no clear answer at all. Finding the right answer is important, but it is not the only goal. As you learn to apply a criminal statute, your criminal law professor will be interested in honing your analytical thinking skills.

The process of taking apart a statute and applying it to the facts of the case is not limited to burglary. Let's do one more example—this time with robbery—just to reinforce the kinds of questions you are going to grapple with. Victims regularly report that they've "been robbed." Here are two common scenarios: First, imagine that Dan pulls out a gun, points it at Victim and says "Give me your money." Second, imagine that Dan breaks into Victim's house at night and steals $1,000 while Victim is out of town. Do these scenarios amount to robbery? Your pre-law school self might be tempted to answer "yes" or "no." But in a Criminal Law class you cannot give either answer, at least initially. In law school, the answer to whether those scenarios are robbery has to be "I can't say yet. I need to see the statute." So here's a typical robbery statute (from Arizona) to help us answer the question:

> A person commits robbery if in the course of taking any property of another from his person or immediate presence and against his will, such person threatens or uses force against any person with intent either to coerce

surrender of property or to prevent resistance to such person taking or retaining property.

Now let's think again about our first scenario in which Dan pointed a gun at Victim and demanded money. Guns can be used to kill or seriously harm people. So pointing a gun at a person surely amounts to a threat of force against another person with the intent to coerce them into giving up their property. Dan is definitely guilty of robbery in Arizona.

But what about the second situation where Dan broke into the house at night and stole the $1,000? That can't be a robbery under the Arizona statute because there is no evidence that Dan threatened force. Indeed, it was impossible to threaten force when no was home. Moreover, even if Victim had been home, there is no evidence that Dan took the property from Victim's "person or immediate presence." Dan could have stolen the money while the Victim was sleeping on another floor of the house. In this situation, Dan is definitely *not* guilty of robbery (though if you flip back a few pages you'll see Dan's actions fall under the classic definition of burglary).

The key takeaway is that your Criminal Law course is not interested in how most people in society describe a situation. Nor is Criminal Law interested in your assumptions or your intuition. You always need to read the statute. And then you will often need to read the court decisions interpreting the statute. And then you will have to think hard about whether the court's reasoning makes sense in light of the statute and the facts of the case. You will repeat this process for other crimes besides robbery and burglary. The goal is for you to practice the skill of statutory interpretation and to hone your analytical thinking. Along the way, you will see how the law has evolved over time.

5. Understanding Defenses: A Separate Concept than the Elements of Crimes

Once you have covered the crimes listed on the syllabus, you will then move on to defenses. Most 1L Criminal Law courses focus on self-defense; duress; intoxication; entrapment; and, of course, insanity. (Spoiler alert: the insanity defense is much more likely to be successful in the movies than it is in the real world.)

Criminal Law professors normally cover defenses at the end of the course because the defenses only come up after the prosecutor has already proven all the elements of a crime. In other words, self-defense does not become an issue if the prosecutor cannot prove that the defendant had the necessary mens rea (e.g. acted purposefully) and committed the actus reus (e.g. pulled the trigger). The prosecutor has the burden to prove each element of the crime beyond a reasonable doubt. Only after that happens does the inquiry turn to whether a defendant can raise a plausible defense such as self-defense or insanity.

As with the elements of the crime, defenses are usually defined by statutes. Courts then fill in the gaps. In other words, the legislature will specify what has to be shown in order for a defendant to qualify for self-defense or the insanity defense. But the statute does not consider every possible scenario. So courts are often called upon to interpret the statutory requirements just as they do for interpreting the elements of the crime.

In recent years, self-defense and stand your ground laws have expanded in scope. Your professor may devote considerable time and attention to this rapidly changing area of law. But you will also spend time on the defenses that tend not to be successful very often. One reason many defenses fail is that they are *affirmative* defenses. This means that the defendant has the burden to show that the defense applies. And with the burden on their shoulders, defendants usually find it tough to prevail.

In analyzing various defenses you will take a historical tour through how the law has changed over time. This is particularly true for the insanity defense. Most people agree that someone who is truly insane should not be convicted of a crime and sent to prison, even if they clearly "did it." The reason is straightforward: even if the defendant intentionally shot the victim, the defendant is not culpable if the defendant was not in his right mind or could not control himself. The idea that mentally ill people should not be criminally responsible seems simple. But that is where the simplicity ends.

Throughout history, legislatures and courts have struggled mightily with figuring out who qualifies as insane. You will see that many states focus on cognitive factors and ask whether a person was suffering from a mental illness that prevented them from *understanding* the difference between right and wrong. Some states also focus on volition and ask whether a defendant suffered from an irresistible impulse and thus could not *control* themselves.

Just as courts and legislatures have struggled with the right standard to apply, so you will struggle in the classroom. Your professor will pick apart the various tests for insanity. Along the way, you should see that there is no clear right answer and that the debate is largely about deciding how broad of an insanity defense a state wants to have. A narrow insanity test leads to few people successfully claiming insanity, while a broader test opens the door more often to defendants being found not guilty by reason of insanity.

In sum, the defenses section of your Criminal Law class (just like the elements of crimes) is about learning statutory analysis and interpretation. The defenses section of the course also calls on you to grapple with public policy questions about who should be held culpable and how much.

6. What Law Are You Learning? The Model Penal Code and Common Law

Some professors will focus on the criminal law of the state where your law school is located. Your whole course might be about New York Criminal Law or the Texas Criminal Code. Most 1L classes are not like this though. Most criminal law textbooks draw on statutes and cases from across the country. You will read cases from many states and the federal courts. You will likely even read a few cases from England because British law was, not surprisingly, a major influence on American law. In other words, most of your Criminal Law course (not to mention your Torts, Property, and Contracts classes) will be a hodgepodge of cases from different times and places.

There is one further wrinkle. Your instructor may spend some time (or even a lot of time) on something called the Model Penal Code. Here is the background on what that is and how you should think about it. In the United States, one of the most esteemed legal organizations is the American Law Institute (the "ALI"). The ALI is composed of prominent judges, lawyers, and law professors, and its members draft model codes and rules as a guide for legislators and policymakers. In 1962, the ALI proposed a Model Penal Code that has been periodically updated ever since. The Model Penal Code (which your professor will probably shorten to "MPC") is a list of provisions that sets out what the lawyers, judges, and law professors in the ALI think the law *should* be. The MPC is not the law of any one state. It is a *model* code.

Your professor may explain to you that some states are "MPC states." This means that those states have adopted large portions of the MPC.

No state has completely adopted the MPC, and some of the specific provisions of the MPC have been rejected by almost every state. Nevertheless, the MPC is very influential, including among criminal law professors. Indeed, the four mens reas we set out in detail above (purpose, knowledge, recklessness, and negligence) are the four mens reas that the MPC uses. So, bottom line, your Criminal Law professor may spend a lot of time focusing on the MPC.

Here is one example of how the MPC might come up in your class so that you can start to think about how it's important. You've probably heard of the crime of statutory rape (when an adult has sex with someone who is too old to consent—usually someone who is a teenager under the age of 18). Many states make statutory rape a strict liability crime, which means that it makes no difference whether the defendant knew (or thought they knew) the child's age. Strict liability means that there is no mens rea and that the defendant can't say "I thought she was over 18." In jurisdictions that make statutory rape a strict liability crime, the defendant is guilty because he had sex with an underage child—end of story.

The MPC mostly rejects the idea of strict liability crimes. The MPC is based on personal culpability, so the idea of holding someone criminally responsible with no mens rea having to be proven is the opposite of what the MPC seeks to do. Instead, the MPC is heavily focused on the what the defendant actually knew or thought. The MPC tends to put more emphasis on what the defendant intended to do, than on the harm he actually caused. So, the MPC doesn't take the same approach to statutory rape as most American jurisdictions. The MPC says that a defendant can escape conviction for statutory rape if he reasonably believed the child was of consenting age.

Statutory rape is just one example. There are many other areas where the MPC differs from the law across the country. For instance, many states break murder down into degrees of seriousness (first-degree murders versus second-degree murder). The MPC rejects the idea of grading murder. You'll also see that the MPC makes it easier to reduce a murder charge to manslaughter than most states are willing to do. The point is not for you to start memorizing what positions the MPC takes and why. You will likely spend plenty of time in class on that. I just flag it here for you to look out for as an important concept you will likely encounter.

Points to Remember

- First-year Criminal Law is about understanding a small number of crimes in a lot of detail.
- Criminal law is heavily driven by statutes. To understand the law, you must read the statute closely.
- Your professor is focusing on a handful of crimes so that you (1) understand those crimes; and (2) can apply the same concepts to other crimes you have not studied in detail.
- Actus reus and mens rea are two building block concepts that make up most criminal statutes. You should focus on the action a defendant has taken and whether she did that action with the mental state (mens rea) listed in the statute.
- Statutes can have lots of different mens reas, but the most common ones are purpose, knowledge, recklessness, and negligence.
- The text of the statute is always the starting point for your analysis, but the text does not always answer the question. You may also have to consider legislative history, logic, fairness, public policy concerns, and other concepts your professor will go over.
- The elements (actus reus, mens rea, and anything else listed in the statute) are the key components of a crime. The prosecution has to prove each element beyond a reasonable doubt in order to convict a defendant.

- If the prosecution has demonstrated all the elements of a crime, you will next consider defenses such as self-defense, intoxication, duress, entrapment, and insanity. Defenses are a separate concept from the elements of the crime.
- Statutes sometimes put the burden on the defendant to prove that a defense applies, which makes it difficult for defendants to claim those defenses.
- You probably will not learn the criminal law of a single state. Instead, your professor and your textbook will focus on cases from around the country. And there is a good chance that your professor will focus on some (or many) of the rules from the Model Penal Code.

CHAPTER 3

Torts

A tort is a fancy word for a wrongful act. Tort law determines when someone is liable for wrongfully causing harm to someone else's person or property. Usually, when we say "harm" we are talking about physical injury. If I push you down a hill and you break your arm, that is a tort. But causing harm to property can also be a tort. If I crash into your car that can also be a tort because I have damaged your personal property.

Not every harm is a tort, though. Accidents happen every day. Sometimes a person is to blame and sometimes bad stuff just happens. The legal system usually does not require a person to pay damages just because they hurt someone. Rather, the focus is usually on whether the defendant acted *wrongfully*, either by committing an intentional tort or acting carelessly (i.e. negligently).[1]

Your Torts class will probably be built around two basic themes: First, the torts system is designed to compensate injured plaintiffs. Most of tort law is about one person accidentally hurting

[1] There is a third category known as "strict liability" where the plaintiff need not demonstrate intentional or negligent conduct. This category is narrower.

someone else. And our society doesn't think it's a good idea to put people in prison for causing accidents. At the same time, we also don't think it's fair to leave injured people with no remedy. So we use the civil justice system to compensate tort victims. The goal here is to look backward at the wrong that happened and to provide "corrective justice" to the plaintiff. Giving people money damages surely isn't a perfect solution to deal with injuries, but it is the best thing our society has figured out.

Second, the torts system is also forward looking. Courts find people liable and impose damages in order to deter others from engaging in dangerous or harmful conduct in the future. Courts choose tort law rules to calibrate the right amount of risk. We don't want people to stop doing productive activities just because there is a chance that they could injure someone. Driving a car is risky but it is valuable to a functioning society. Some risks are worth it! So the torts system doesn't impose legal liability and damages for every sort of injury that happens in the world. Instead, the tort system tries to deter people from engaging in behavior that is *excessively* risky. In other words, the goal is not to deter all risk. The goal is optimal deterrence.

As you study Torts, you are going to cover a lot of concepts that often seem mushy. Students often complain that the law they learn in Torts is kind of amorphous and unclear. Students will sometimes say that the main thing they learned in Torts was that people are supposed to "act reasonably." To some extent, this is true. There is going to be a lot of "reasonableness" analysis in your Torts class. Nevertheless, we can break your Torts course down into smaller concepts with at least some rules. Let's get started by outlining the four topics your professor is likely to spend the most time on—intentional torts, negligence, strict liability, and damages.

1. *Intentional Torts*: Sometimes a person acts terribly and intentionally causes harm to another person or

their property. We call these intentional torts, and the main ones are:

- Battery
- Assault
- False Imprisonment
- Intentional Infliction of Emotional Distress
- Trespass to Land
- Harm to Property (trespass to chattels and conversion)

2. *Negligence*: This is the big enchilada. The vast majority of your Torts class will be about negligence. While most people would never harm people or property intentionally, there are a lot of careless people out there. Whether they are drunk, uncoordinated, or just bad drivers, people cause accidents all the time. The question is when accidents should give rise to compensation. To figure that out, your negligence discussion is going to focus on four main concepts that we will explore in more detail later:

   - Did the defendant owe a duty of care to the plaintiff?
   - Can the plaintiff show that the defendant breached the duty of care?
   - Did the defendant's negligence factually cause the plaintiff's injury?
   - Was the injury foreseeable enough to hold the plaintiff responsible?

3. *Strict Liability*: There are some situations where the law does not require a plaintiff to prove that the defendant caused harm intentionally or negligently. The law holds people (or corporations) responsible just because they caused something bad to happen, regardless of intent. The most common scenario involves defective products. When a merchant sells a defective product that causes harm, the plaintiff can recover damages even without showing the merchant was careless. Another strict liability scenario you'll likely see is associated with abnormally dangerous activities such as the operation of chemical plants.
4. *Damages*: When there has been a tort, how much money does the defendant have to pay the plaintiff? Your professor will explain the difference between compensatory damages (to compensate the victim) and punitive damages (to punish the defendant). You will also learn about limits on damages, such as the duty to mitigate.

Okay, let's get a little more specific!

1. Intentional Torts

The first step in an intentional torts question is figuring out whether the defendant acted intentionally. Intent doesn't require a showing that the defendant was a terrible person. Instead, the question is whether the defendant had the purpose to cause something to happen, or whether the defendant knew to a substantial certainty that the thing would happen. Every one of the intentional torts requires that the plaintiff first demonstrate that the defendant acted with intent—either with purpose or knowledge.

The next step after demonstrating intent is figuring out which intentional tort we are dealing with and whether the elements of that intentional tort are met. You can break the intentional torts down into two buckets—those where a person is injured and those where property is harmed. Here are the key intentional torts and a brief description of each:

Intentional Injury to a Person

1. Battery is the intentional infliction of harmful or offensive bodily contact. In short, the plaintiff intentionally touched the defendant in some way and caused harm or offense. Harm is easy to demonstrate—any kind of physical injury will usually do. Hitting someone is a battery. So is pulling out a person's chair as they are about to sit down, even though you meant it as a joke. Showing that conduct is "offensive" can be trickier. If you spit in my face, that is probably offensive. If you poke me in the chest repeatedly while yelling at me, that is also probably offensive. Both of those situations would offend a reasonable person's sense of dignity. But just tapping me on the shoulder to ask for directions probably doesn't suffice, even if (unbeknownst to you) I really hate it when people tap me on the shoulder. To figure out whether conduct is offensive, you will ask whether a reasonable person would have been offended.

2. Assault is when the defendant intentionally creates the impression of an imminent battery. If the defendant raises his hand as if he is going to strike the plaintiff (but never does so), that is an assault. The reason is that the victim would be put in "apprehension" of harmful or offensive conduct. Once again, we are focused on what a reasonable plaintiff would have thought. If it was obvious that the defendant was just kidding and would not really have hit the plaintiff, then no assault occurred. Additionally, remember that the threat of

striking a person must be "imminent." If I tell you that I plan to smack you in the face after I finish watching every single episode of Law and Order,[2] that is not imminent.

3. False Imprisonment is confining a person against their will in a particular area. To prevail, the plaintiff has to show that the plaintiff knew he was locked in that area. And the plaintiff has to have no way out. Blocking one of two exits to a room is not false imprisonment.

4. Intentional Infliction of Emotional Distress is a tort where the defendant intentionally engages in extreme and outrageous conduct that causes emotional distress to the plaintiff. Figuring out what is "extreme and outrageous" can be difficult, and your professor will likely use hypotheticals and the Socratic Method to help you draw some lines in this murky area.

Intentional Harm to Property

5. Trespass to Land occurs when a defendant intentionally enters the land of another. In addition to obvious cases of a person walking onto another's land, you may study cases about a defendant throwing an object onto another's land or even cases where the defendant dug a mine or tunnel underneath another person's land. The plaintiff need not prove physical damage to the property. The harm is simply that the defendant trespassed on the land.

6. Trespass to Personal Property: Personal property is moveable property such as your car or your cell phone. There are two kinds of trespasses to personal property: (A) trespass to chattels and (B) conversion. Trespass to chattels is the junior varsity version. When a defendant minorly interferes with your use of personal property that is a trespass to chattels. An

[2] You probably didn't know that there are over 500 episodes of Law and Order. Now you do.

example would be if I took your cell phone without permission, used it to make a phone call, and then gave it back. Conversion is the more serious tort. A defendant converts property when she creates serious obstacles that interfere with my use of the property, essentially treating the property as her own. So if the defendant took my cell phone and wouldn't return it for a week, or if she smashed the phone so that the glass was shattered and unusable, she would have converted the property. As you can imagine, the line between trespass to chattels and conversion can be blurry and your professor may use the Socratic Method to force you to draw distinctions.

2. Negligence

Negligence is the big topic in Torts. As we said at the outset, our society does not usually put people in jail just because they accidentally hurt someone else. But it is fair to have the person who caused the accident pay for the harm, rather than having the victim pay. So the tort of negligence fills that role.

At the outset, it's important to understand that the word "negligence" can mean two different things. First, negligence is a state of mind. As we discussed in the Criminal Law chapter, people can act negligently when they should have been aware of an unjustifiable risk. In other words, negligence is the mental state of being careless. Second, negligence can be the type of lawsuit a plaintiff is filing. When someone asks the plaintiff what type of case they are bringing, the plaintiff would say "a negligence case." Although you will talk about negligence in terms of the defendant's mental state, your Torts class will mostly be about negligence as a type of lawsuit.

And negligence will be the big topic in your Torts class. Not only will negligence occupy the most class sessions, it will also be the murkiest topic. Negligence law is set out at "high level of generality." What does that mean? For the most part, the same set of negligence rules applies to car accidents and brain surgery and everything in between. This means that there are few specific rules and instead a lot of generalized (and seemingly vague) standards. Be prepared for a lot of discussion about what is "reasonable" and what is not.

To understand why negligence law often seems so vague, I want you to think about the million things a driver could be doing when they get into a car accident. They could be changing the radio station, adjusting the temperature, eating something, talking with a passenger, watching another car go by, or thinking about what they are going to eat for dinner Would any of those *automatically* be negligent? No. People safely change the radio station and adjust the temperature while driving all the time. Is there a magic list somewhere of what behaviors are negligent and which aren't? No. Instead, whether behavior is negligent depends on the circumstances. If I turn my head just for a second to see a police car drive by that's probably not negligent. But if I turn around 180 degrees to stare at Taylor Swift driving down the road and stop looking in front of me that can be negligent. Negligence is in the details.

A quick comparison to criminal law should help to bring all of this into focus. To be guilty of burglary, you have to break and enter the dwelling house of another at night with an intent to commit a felony inside. That is a very specific rule. To be liable for negligence you have to do something unreasonably in a way that causes harm. That's a very general rule. In other words, the tort of negligence is set at a high level of generality so that it can cover a lot of behavior, as opposed to burglary or any other criminal offense which covers very specific behavior. And we need to go case-by-case with lots of different sets of facts to figure out what amounts to negligence and what doesn't. Because we have a general rule that might or might not include the millions of scenarios that come up every day, there is a lot of vagueness in the negligence rules.

But don't get discouraged. Even though negligence can seem amorphous, there are four clear steps your professor will walk you through to analyze a negligence claim: (1) Duty of Care; (2) Breach; (3) Factual Causation; and (4) Proximate Causation.[3] Let's go through the different steps of a negligence analysis.

a. *The Duty of Care*

Not everyone who gets hurt is entitled to relief. That's because the first step in any negligence case is to determine whether the defendant owed the plaintiff a duty of care. So let's start with the defendant and her actions. We like to say that the United States is a "free country" and that people can do whatever they want. But that's not entirely true. Tort law imposes a duty on people to behave in a way that reduces risk to others. We have to take some precautions to make sure we don't hurt other people. The question is "Which precautions?" Once again, Tort law does not give us a clear list in advance. Instead, we have a duty to behave reasonably under the circumstances.

For instance, there is usually no duty to rescue another person. By contrast, if you are in a special relationship (such as parent to a child) there is a duty to protect the vulnerable person. Landowners have a duty of care to have safe conditions for people they invite onto their land. But landowners usually don't have a duty of care to make things safe for trespassers. You get the idea. If your professor raises these specific rules, you should be sure to focus on them.

---

[3] There is also the question of damages, but we'll leave that until the very end of this chapter.

b. Breach of the Duty of Care

Let's imagine that I've started powerwalking on busy city streets as my primary form of exercise.[4] I like to swing my arms out sideways while I walk because I think it improves my workout. There's no law that says I can't swing my arms to the side while I walk. But I have a duty to behave prudently and to use reasonable care under the circumstances. If it is 3:00am and no one is around, that probably means I can swing my arms any way I like. But if I am walking through the middle of a crowded city at lunchtime then I can't swing my arms too far because I will likely hit other people. I have a duty to behave reasonably under the circumstances.

Imagine that I hit someone while walking. The next question is whether I have breached my duty of care. Of course, it would be nice to have a clear rule here that says I can only swing my arms out one foot from my body. Then everyone would know what they're allowed to do and what they can't do. But there are no such rules. After all, how far I can swing my arms would depend on circumstances such as how wide the streets are and how many people are walking through them. So we have to come back to reasonableness.

One way to figure out whether I was unreasonably swinging my arms too far to the side is custom. How do people in this city normally walk down the street? Beyond that, professors love to talk about the famous formula that Judge Learned Hand[5] invented for determining reasonableness. That formula is $B < P \times L$. It stands for Burden is less than Probability times Loss. Basically, the formula asks what the burden or cost on the defendant was of taking better precautions. And on the other side of the equation, it asks what was the likelihood that a bad event would have occurred and how much

---

4 Don't make fun. Middle age will happen to you at some point too. Trust me.

5 Judge Learned Hand was a famous judge who you will hear about multiple times in law school. And yes, that was his real name.

damage it would have caused. In short, the Hand formula is a cost-benefit analysis. When the individual could have avoided the damages by doing something that cost less than the damages caused by the injury, they should do it. But when the individual would have to spend a lot of money to prevent a small risk, it would not be reasonable to take precautions.

If you're like me, the Hand formula is hard to understand in the abstract, so let's do an example. Imagine that a grocery store has water pipes in the ceiling and that the pipe over Aisle 7 has started to leak. The leak leaves a small puddle of water that is hard to see. It would cost the store $300 to have a plumber go up to the ceiling and fix the pipes to stop the leak. That's the burden or cost. On the other side of the equation, the chances that someone would slip and fall because of some drops of water are low—let's say 1 in 100. That's the probability. But if someone slips and falls they may seriously hurt themselves and need $40,000 in back surgery. That would be the loss. Now let's fill in the formula B ($300) < P (1%) × L ($40,000). And to make it easier, let's do the math: B ($300) < PL ($400). It would cost the grocery store $300 to fix the leak, but the probable loss (injury) from the leak is $400. In short, it would cost less to fix the leak than the probability of the loss. Under those circumstances, it was unreasonable not to fix the leak. The grocery store has breached its duty of care by acting unreasonably.

Of course, the Hand Formula is just a guide. Cases involve real people, and the facts are often much more complicated. Imagine that the grocery store didn't call the plumber but that it did put up a sign warning people about the puddle of water. That would reduce the risk of injury and thus change the equation. At the end of the day, the question of breach still comes down to reasonableness.

In addition to the general reasonableness analysis, your professor will likely also focus on some special situations. You are likely to focus on medical professionals in particular. Here, we don't ask what a reasonable person would have done during brain surgery. We ask what other brain surgeons would have done. In other words, what is the custom of the profession? We don't focus on what the best brain surgeon would have done. Or what the highest-paid surgeon with the fanciest office in New York City would have done. We ask what the going rate is for brain surgeons across the country.

c. Factual Causation: The "but for" Test

It is not enough that the plaintiff shows that the defendant had a duty of care and breached it. In other words, we need more than the defendant simply acting negligently. We also need the negligence to have factually caused the plaintiff's injury. This is usually phrased as a "but for" test: But for the defendant's breach, the plaintiff would not have been injured.

Consider again the leaking pipe in the grocery store that left a puddle of water. In most instances, the factual causation question is easy. The plaintiff stepped in the puddle and fell as a result. We would phrase that as "but for the grocery store leaving the puddle of water there, the plaintiff would not have slipped and been injured." Pretty simple.

But the facts might be more complicated. Let's say that the plaintiff was older and walked with a cane. And let's also say that the plaintiff was talking to his granddaughter as he was walking through Aisle 7. The granddaughter said she really wanted to buy some cookies. Having just passed the cookies, the plaintiff turned around quickly—probably a little too quickly for someone his age. And right around the puddle, the plaintiff fell and hurt himself. Can we still say that the puddle of water was the factual cause of the accident? Maybe it was. Or maybe the grandfather fell because he turned too quickly and lost his balance—in other words, he would have fallen in just the same way even if the floor had been dry. A jury will have to sort out whether the plaintiff still would have fallen but for the water being on the floor.

d. *Proximate Causation: Lack of Foreseeability Cuts off Liability*

Even if there is a duty of care, a breach, and factual ("but for") causation, the plaintiff's claim can still fail if there is no proximate causation. Proximate causation is the idea that we have to cut off liability at some point when it has become too disconnected from the negligence. If the injury is too indirect, or if it is not a foreseeable result of the defendant's misconduct it doesn't make sense to hold the defendant responsible. Proximate cause is basically just a policy statement that we shouldn't hold the defendant liable in certain situations. Proximate cause is a terrible name for the concept because students sometimes confuse it with factual ("but for") causation. But the term proximate cause has been around for generations, and it isn't going to change. So we have to just roll with it. Let's do an example to help us understand.

Imagine that I am teaching my class and trying to keep the students engaged. I am waiving my arms wildly all over the place in an effort to keep everyone's attention. I have plenty of room to stand away from the students in the front row, but I'm kind of excited about teaching negligence law, so I get right up close to the front row. And I accidentally hit a student in the face with my arm.

It should be pretty clear that I owed the student a duty of care not to swing my arm so close to her face and that I've breached that duty. Thankfully, the student isn't too hurt, and she gets up to go outside for some fresh air. The student walks down the stairs, across the lobby, and out the front door of the law school. Once she's outside though, a freak accident occurs. A construction crane drops a piece of concrete which lands on her and breaks her foot.

But for me hitting the student with my arm, she would never have gone outside at that moment and the concrete never would have fallen on her and broken her foot. So I am the "but for" cause—the factual cause—of her broken foot. But am I the proximate cause? Does it make sense to hold me responsible for something so far removed from swinging my arms too close to her head in a classroom? Remember, my negligence was in the classroom. And now the student has left that room, walked down the stairs, across the lobby, and out the front door. It seems pretty far removed from my actions.

To give you another example, imagine that the student whom I hit with my arm was the smartest student in the whole law school. She had already lined up a job with the most prestigious law firm in the nation where she would get paid a huge salary after graduating. But after I swung my arm into her in the front row, she walked out the front door of the law school and never came back. She was traumatized by being struck in the face and decided never to go back to law school. As a result, she never graduated and thus couldn't work at the fancy law firm job and earn the huge salary. Can she sue me not just for the minor injury caused by my flailing arms, but also from the loss of her law firm salary? Almost certainly not. There is a lack of proximate cause.

The main test for proximate cause is foreseeability. The plaintiff has to show that her injuries are the foreseeable consequence of the defendant's negligent conduct. If the injuries are too remote in time or in connection to the defendant's negligence they are not foreseeable and thus are not proximate. The core idea here is that the defendant's liability has to end at some point. Once again, the rules are amorphous.

Court decisions on proximate cause effectively amount to policy choices. But remember the principles of tort law. We are trying to fairly compensate plaintiffs for their injuries, not to give them extra money. And we are trying to find the right level of deterrence—not too much and not too little. We don't want to create a rule that over-deters me from getting excited in class. If we had such a rule, I might over-correct my behavior. Not only will I stop swinging my arms around, but I might decide to always stand behind the podium and just read my class notes aloud in a monotone voice. That overreaction—what we could call over-deterrence—would be problematic because now my class will be boring and students will learn less. Tort law is about striking the right balance, and proximate cause helps to do that.

3. Strict Liability

So far we've talked about intentional torts and negligent torts. Intentional torts involve people purposefully or knowingly causing harm. Negligent torts are for scenarios where the defendant didn't intend to hurt anyone but still behaved carelessly. Both of these torts involve "fault." Not only did the defendants cause harm but we can point to bad behavior (either intentional or negligent).

What about cases where the defendant wasn't even negligent though? The defendant acted reasonably, exercised the right amount of care, but something bad still happened anyway. Holding the defendant responsible in this situation is called "strict liability."

Strict liability is not common in criminal law because it seems unfair to send someone to jail when they completely lacked any mens rea. Historically, strict liability was also uncommon in tort law. The logic went that if the plaintiff couldn't show the defendant to have been negligent then society should not force the defendant to pay for the injury. Over time however, strict liability has crept into tort law. To be sure, negligence is still the biggest category of tort law, followed by intentional torts as a runner-up. But there are some strict liability torts doctrines you should know. Here are the two most important.

First, tort law will allow for strict liability when the defendant engaged in an abnormally dangerous activity. When an activity is uncommon and so dangerous that even reasonable care won't prevent the risk, courts are sometimes willing to apply strict liability. In these cases, the defendant's lack of negligence is irrelevant. The defendant is responsible even if it acted reasonably. I say "it" because a classic example of abnormally dangerous activity would be a chemical company making extremely toxic substances. Here, strict liability is basically saying "if you choose to engage in such inherently dangerous behavior, you have to pay for the injuries that result."

Second, manufacturing defects that cause personal injury or property damage are also subject to a strict liability standard. To understand why, think of the thousands of parts that go into building an automobile. If the car is defective, the odds are that the car manufacturer was negligent somewhere along the line in building the car. But with such a complicated piece of equipment, it can be difficult for a plaintiff to demonstrate how the car manufacturer failed to exercise reasonable care in assembling the car. In other words, it would be really hard for the plaintiff to prove that the manufacturer was negligent. And that seems unfair to the regular person on the street who paid a lot of money for a broken piece of equipment. Moreover, the manufacturer is better positioned to put safeguards in place to reduce the risk of defects happening. So even if it is a little unfair to hold the manufacturer strictly liable, that is still better than letting the unfairness fall on the regular old person buying a car.

Of course, just because a product is not working as the plaintiff hoped does not mean the manufacturer is always liable. Courts still require the plaintiff to demonstrate that the product is defective and that the product had not been altered by someone after the manufacturer sold it. Additionally, a plaintiff only gets to claim strict liability if they are using the product for its intended purpose. If a plaintiff claims the oven in their kitchen is defective because it will not heat their house in the winter that strict liability claim is going to lose.

4. Damages

There are two categories of damages in civil suits: compensatory damages and punitive damages. Compensatory damages are to "make the victim whole." If I totally destroy your car, which was worth $20,000, the compensatory damages would be $20,000. Punitive damages are not about compensating the plaintiff, but instead are about punishing the defendant for egregious behavior. Because most torts cases are about negligence—run of the mill carelessness rather than egregious misconduct—punitive damages are pretty rare in torts cases. So let's focus our attention on compensatory damages.

Let's take a standard car accident to think about the types of compensatory damages at issue. First, if I crashed into you, I probably harmed your car. I will likely owe you money for the property damage. If the car can be repaired, I will owe you the cost of the repair. If the car is totaled, I will owe you the fair market value of the car.

Second, there is a good chance I have physically hurt you. Let's imagine that you broke your leg in the car accident. You probably had medical bills shortly after the accident. And you may have future medical bills as you continue to deal with your injuries. Additionally, you probably missed work and can claim damages for lost wages. Finally, you may be entitled to damages for pain and suffering. All of these injuries can fall into the category of compensatory damages.

Figuring out the amount of damages requires evidence. To be compensated for medical bills and car repairs, the plaintiff will have to submit bills and receipts. To be compensated for pain and suffering, the plaintiff will likely have to testify about his injuries.

Medical bills and pain and suffering can lead to surprisingly huge damages awards in some cases. The reason is that the defendant takes the plaintiff as she finds him. This is the so-called "eggshell skull" rule. Some people are very frail, even if they don't look it. And they may suffer more extensive injuries than the average person. Even though most of tort law is about the "reasonable" person, we do not award damages based on how injured the average person would have been. Instead, the damages amount is based on the injuries the victim actually suffered. So if I negligently bang into a 23-year-old law student and cause him to tumble down a hill, we don't ask how injured the average 23-year old would be. We ask about the actual victim. And if that victim had an unusual medical condition with frail bones that led to more extensive injuries, that's too bad for the defendant. You take your victim as you find them, and courts award the actual damages suffered.

It's not all bad news for defendants though. There are legal doctrines that reduce the amount of damages a plaintiff can collect. Remember, we don't want to over-compensate victims. We want to make them whole by putting them in a place similar to where they would have been in had the accident not occurred.

First, the torts system limits damages by imposing a "duty to mitigate" on plaintiffs. If your broken leg caused you to lose your job as a store clerk (where you had to stand a lot) you would be entitled to damages for lost wages. But that would not mean you never have to work again. The victim has a duty to mitigate their damages by looking for another job.

A second limit on damages is "discounting." A virtue of the torts system is that it resolves everything at once. So, if your broken leg is going to prevent you from working for the next 10 years, we don't come back to court every year and assess your situation. Instead, a single lawsuit resolves the issue once and for all. A jury might look at the evidence, see that you make $50,000 per year and decide that you will lose all of that income for the next 10 years. But giving you $500,000 right now would be over-compensation. If the court gave you $500,000 tomorrow, you could invest it in the stock market or even just a basic savings account. It would grow to well more than $500,000 over time. That is over-compensation. So courts have to discount damages awards to account for the time value of money.

Third, in recent years, states have passed laws imposing damages caps. For instance, some states are skeptical of pain and suffering damages and have set limits on how much a plaintiff can collect.

Fourth, a defendant may be entitled to "indemnification" from other parties. For instance, imagine that a car manufacturer is forced to pay $100,000 in damages because the brakes failed and the driver was injured. The car manufacturer likely got the brake parts from another company. If the brake parts were defective, the car manufacturer can seek to be reimbursed or "indemnified" by the brake parts company for the money it paid to the driver.

Points To Remember

- A tort is a physical harm or property damage.
- Just because someone caused an injury does not mean they committed a tort. Torts usually require a person to have behaved wrongfully.

- The goal of tort law is to compensate plaintiffs for their injuries and to deter future unreasonably dangerous activities. The goal is not to eliminate all risk.
- Intentional torts require a person to act purposefully or knowingly.
- Most injuries happen as a result of carelessness, not intentional misconduct. As such, most of your Torts class will be about negligence. Negligence is a cause of action—a type of lawsuit.
- Negligence is a very general cause of action. The same basic rules apply to car crashes and failed brain surgeries.
- The key concepts for understanding a negligence claim are (1) duty of care; (2) breach of the duty of care; (3) factual (but for) causation; and (4) proximate causation.
- Analyzing the duty of care and breach focuses on what an objectively reasonable person would have done under the same circumstances.
- Proximate causation is a legal principle (a policy) designed to cut off liability when it becomes too far removed from the negligent acts. When an injury is not a foreseeable result of negligence there is no proximate cause.
- In a few situations, courts use strict liability to hold people or companies responsible even though they did not act intentionally or negligently.
- Courts use strict liability for abnormally dangerous activities and for manufacturing defects.
- Tort law is primarily about compensatory damages to make the victim whole, not punitive damages to punish the defendant.
- Damages are determined based on the victim's actual injuries, not the injuries that an average person would have suffered

under the circumstances. The defendant takes their victim as they found them.

- There are legal doctrines that limit damages awards such as the plaintiff's duty to mitigate damages, discounting to present value, statutory damages caps, and indemnification.

CHAPTER 4

Civil Procedure

Your other 1L classes are about the rights and duties that people have. For instance, in Property you will learn about interests in land ownership. In Torts, you will study your duties to others, particularly not to harm people or property. All of those classes introduce you to *substantive* rights and responsibilities that you possess. Civil Procedure, by contrast, is about *procedural* rights. Civil Procedure is about how you can go to court and enforce your substantive rights.

People can't just show up in a random court one day and have their case heard immediately. Instead, you have to find the correct court to bring your lawsuit, write down your complaint in enough detail to show you have a viable claim, serve notice on the defendant, and exchange information with the other party so that everyone has access to the facts (i.e. discovery). Civil Procedure is about understanding how the process works.

Before we go any further, let me make a confession. I didn't really understand Civil Procedure very well when I was in law school. Sure, I could tell you the standard for when a court had jurisdiction. And I could answer questions about the various types of discovery.

But I definitely didn't get the big picture of how everything fits together.

The big challenge in your Civil Procedure class will be figuring out how the puzzle pieces fit together. For example, early in a case the defendant can move to dismiss the case for lack of jurisdiction. Around that time, (but sometimes later on in the process), the defendant can try to add additional parties to the lawsuit. Or the defendant can file counterclaims against the plaintiff. At some point, the parties will probably have to exchange lots of documents, answer each other's questions, and have their witnesses be deposed. They might fight over what law applies to their case. You may struggle with understanding how everything fits together.

Moreover, even if you see how the pieces fit together, it is easy to get lost in the details. There are so many doctrinal rabbit holes in Civil Procedure that it is really easy to get yourself tied in knots. You've probably heard the expression that you shouldn't "miss the forest for the trees." It is really easy in Civil Procedure to get so caught up in the trees that you don't step back and look at the forest.

So here is your first piece of practical advice: You are probably going to be confused in your Civil Procedure during the first few weeks. So, don't panic. It will be okay. Be patient.

The second challenge of Civil Procedure is that the source of the law will be much different from that in your other classes. In Torts, Property and (mostly in) Contracts you will be going over common law rules that have been developed by judges over hundreds of years. You won't learn the law of any one state. Instead, you will read cases from all over the country and from different time periods. You'll be learning big picture legal principles. Civil Procedure is different. In most Civil Procedure courses, students focus on learning the *federal* rules of civil procedure. And you will be doing that by reading not just court decisions but also federal statutes and a detailed set of rules that are actually called the "Federal Rules of Civil Procedure." Those rules are dense and technical. For many topics, the starting point will not be a judicial decision but instead the relevant rule from the Federal Rules of Civil Procedure—the "FRCP."

Since your Civil Procedure course is based in part on the FRCP, let's get something important (and unpleasant) on the table early. When your professor assigns specific rules in the FRCP, you *must* read them. And you have to read them carefully. So, don't just read the cases. Your professor will expect you to read and understand the FRCP, even if the particular rules are not discussed in any of the assigned cases.

A third challenge for Civil Procedure is that some of the rules are complicated and technical. This course requires a lot of attention to detail. So be prepared to re-read your textbook and your class notes.

There's no way we can cover even a fraction of the FRCP in this short chapter. And, let's be honest, you are not reading this book for the nitty gritty details of civil procedure. But this book can help you to zoom out and understand the big concepts. So, let's break your Civil Procedure course down into the seven most important topics you'll cover in class so that you can start to see the big picture:

1. Personal Jurisdiction: Did the defendant have enough contact with this jurisdiction that we can make them defend a lawsuit here?
2. Subject Matter Jurisdiction: Does a federal court have authority to hear this *type* of claim? In other words, what is the case about?
3. The Erie Doctrine: Which law applies, state or federal?

4. Pleadings: Has the plaintiff alleged facts that actually amount to a legal claim? And does the defendant have any arguments to move to dismiss the case at the very beginning?

5. Discovery: What kinds of information can the plaintiff and the defendant get from each other and how do they get it? Discovery involves document requests, depositions, specific questions called interrogatories, and requests by each side that the other admit or deny certain facts. Along the way, the parties may claim the attorney-client privilege and something called the work product doctrine to fight discovery requests.

6. Joinder: Many lawsuits involve a plaintiff suing a defendant based on one claim. But what if the plaintiff or the defendant want to add more parties? And what if the plaintiff or the defendant want to add more claims? Can everything and everyone be part of one lawsuit?

7. Preclusion: If some matters have been decided in a prior lawsuit, can they be litigated all over again? Or are the parties bound by prior decisions in other courts?

Let's explain each of these topics in a little more detail (but not too much!).

1. Personal Jurisdiction

You will probably spend a lot of time in your Civil Procedure class learning how to determine if there is a "personal jurisdiction" in a given case. Personal jurisdiction raises the question of whether a court has power over this particular defendant. That's why it is called *personal* jurisdiction. To answer that question, courts typically ask whether the defendant has enough ties to the jurisdiction that it is permissible to sue them there.

Here's a simple example to get started: You sue me for breach of contract in Nevada because a product I sold you is allegedly defective. You live in Las Vegas. Even though I live in Virginia, I sell my products in Nevada and fly into Las Vegas four times a year to meet with my clients. I also employ two sales representatives who live and work in Nevada. It's pretty clear that I have extensive ties to Nevada. So if I claim a lack of personal jurisdiction in Nevada, I am going to lose. It's not even a close call.

But let's make it more challenging. Let's say, again, that I live in Virginia, that you live in Las Vegas, and that you want to bring your breach of contract claim against me in Nevada. But this time, assume my business is tiny. I don't fly to Las Vegas for work. I don't have any sales representatives in Nevada. Indeed, I don't even ship my products to Nevada. You bought one of my products in California (where I do sell things), and you drove home to Nevada with my product. My only connection to Las Vegas is that I went there on a vacation seven years ago to see a Cirque du Soleil show. Is there personal jurisdiction for me in Nevada?

You'll learn that the test for personal jurisdiction is whether the defendant had "minimum contacts" with the jurisdiction. Key factors include whether the contacts are "related" or "unrelated" to the subject of the lawsuit and whether those contacts are "isolated" or whether they are "continuous and systematic." You can probably guess that my vacation trip to Vegas was unrelated and isolated and thus does not create personal jurisdiction.

So now we've done two easy cases on both ends of the personal jurisdiction spectrum. Let's try one in the middle. Imagine that I sell most of my products in California, so that's where all of my sales representatives live and work. Even though I don't have an office or any staff in Las Vegas, I will ship products there if a buyer contacts me requesting it. I do less than 1% of my business in the state of Nevada. Imagine that my product broke and hurt someone in Las Vegas, which is why the plaintiff is suing me. Finally, forget about the vacation I took in Las Vegas seven years ago. My flight was cancelled, and in fact I have never set foot in the state of Nevada in my entire life.

It's now a closer call whether I have enough contact with Nevada to be subject to personal jurisdiction there. But the answer is probably "yes." Nevada has an interest in protecting its citizens from harm, and my product allegedly caused harm in Nevada. And you better believe that if a Nevada resident contracted for my product and didn't pay that I would try to use the Nevada courts to enforce my contract. So the courts would say that I have "purposefully availed" myself of the Nevada forum.

It's too early for you to start worrying about memorizing terms like "purposeful availment" or "minimum contacts." Indeed, there are lots of other personal jurisdiction doctrines that I have left out (such as whether the forum is unreasonable under the circumstances). The point is not for you to start learning the details of Civil Procedure from this book. Instead, you should start to see the kinds of jurisdiction questions your professor will make you grapple with in your Civil Procedure course.

2. Subject Matter Jurisdiction

We've seen that personal jurisdiction is about whether a court has power over a particular person. Subject matter jurisdiction raises the question of whether a court has power over a particular *type* of case. Here you are focusing on the claims in the lawsuit—for instance a tort action from a car crash, a patent dispute, or a breach of contract claim—and asking whether the court is authorized by law to hear that type of claim.

In state court, this question is usually pretty easy. Imagine that I crash my car into your car in Nevada. It's pretty clear that you can sue me in the Nevada state courts because Nevada's laws very clearly allow parties to bring tort lawsuits in state courts. But most of your Civil Procedure course will be about *federal* court, not state court. And federal courts have limited jurisdiction. If you walk into federal court in all of its majesty, you don't usually see a lot of car accident cases. The reason is that (except in unusual cases) federal law does not authorize federal courts to hear run-of-the-mill car accident cases. So subject matter jurisdiction is about determining whether the court has authority to hear the *type* of case. If there is no subject matter jurisdiction, the court has to throw out the case.

There are two main ways that federal courts get jurisdiction over a case: (A) when Congress has passed a law to give courts "federal question jurisdiction" or (B) when "diversity jurisdiction" exists. The "federal question" cases are pretty easy, and most professors won't spend a ton of time on them. Two easy examples are patent cases and bankruptcy cases. The United States Congress decided long ago that those two areas of law are complicated and that they don't want states mucking around with them. So there are special federal laws for patent and bankruptcy cases and those laws provide that disputes go to federal court. Your professor may draw your attention to some other federal questions, but probably not many.

The harder jurisdiction topic is "diversity" jurisdiction, and this is where you will spend more time. In Civil Procedure, the word diversity isn't focused on the topics we normally associate with that word. There will be no discussion of racial, gender, or sexual orientation diversity. Diversity jurisdiction is about *geographic* diversity.

There's a long history in the United States of not trusting state courts. One instance when we are skeptical of state courts is when one of the parties is from out of the state. Imagine that someone from New Jersey visits Idaho for the day and is rear-ended by a local Idaho driver. Idaho has a small population and a close-knit community. As you might imagine, people from New Jersey are not always beloved in Idaho (or in many other places).[1] Is it possible that our out-of-state New Jersey plaintiff is going to get a raw deal in Idaho *state* court? Maybe. Would the New Jersey plaintiff be treated more fairly in *federal* court, which is supposed to be the fairest forum of them all? Perhaps.

The idea of diversity jurisdiction is to let our New Jersey driver sue in federal court. To be specific about it, diversity jurisdiction permits a plaintiff to file a lawsuit in federal court if the plaintiff and the defendant are from two different states and the amount at issue in the lawsuit is worth more than $75,000.

Here's a simple example. If you and I live in Las Vegas and I crash my car into you, I can only sue you in state court. There is no diversity jurisdiction because we both live in Nevada. But what if I live in Virginia (true) and went on vacation to Las Vegas (which I love to do), and I crash my rental car into you two blocks from your home in Nevada. Now there is "complete diversity" because we are from different states. You can use diversity jurisdiction to sue me in federal court if you claim more than $75,000 in damages.

You might be thinking, "Diversity jurisdiction seems simple. How is this a core topic?" Well the diversity problems can become much more complicated. What if I crashed into you because the brakes on my rental car failed. So you decide to sue not just me, but also the car rental car company for failing to properly maintain the car. Now imagine that the rental car company is incorporated in Delaware (that's where the company's lawyers filed the paperwork to create the company). Also imagine that the company

---

1 As someone born and raised in New Jersey, I can attest to this. Whether it is for a good reason, I won't say.

rents most of its cars in California. And finally, note that the rental car company's main headquarters is in Nevada. Now, we have to ask if there is complete diversity of parties if a Nevada plaintiff sues a Virginia citizen and also a company that has ties to Delaware, California, and Nevada. You should now see how diversity jurisdiction can become quite complicated. As you study diversity jurisdiction, you'll learn the rules about a company's "principal places of business" and what counts as "complete diversity."

3. The Erie Doctrine

The Erie doctrine (which is named after a Supreme Court case) is probably the most feared (or maybe we should say "most hated") part of Civil Procedure. When you want to tell a classmate you're having a bad day, you'll probably make a joke about the Erie doctrine. And everyone will understand. I'll leave the torturous details of the Erie doctrine to your professor and just give you a simple overview.

A key question in any lawsuit is which law should apply. In state court, the answer is simple: the law of that state applies. In federal court, you might assume that the court always applies federal law. And that is sometimes the case. Recall that a federal court can have subject matter jurisdiction based on a "federal question." We talked about patent cases and bankruptcy cases as two examples of Congress creating a federal question. When there is a federal question, the federal court will apply the federal law. A federal court hearing a patent case will apply federal patent law. That's pretty simple.

Now the hard part. What do we do when the federal court is hearing a diversity case. Remember the example where I flew from my home in Virginia to Las Vegas, rented a car while on vacation, and crashed into your car. You could file a lawsuit in federal court based on diversity jurisdiction. (I'm from Virginia and you're from

Nevada.) But even though we'll be in federal court, there isn't a detailed set of federal car crash laws. Should federal courts just make up a new set of rules to govern our car crash lawsuit? And even if the court could make up new federal rules, would it be fair to apply federal law when I probably caused the crash by violating the traffic laws of Nevada?

Under the Erie doctrine, the federal court will apply the state law (Nevada law in our hypothetical) to all *substantive* issues. So if the question in the case is whether I was driving recklessly or exceeding the speed limit, we would look to Nevada law, even though we are in federal court.

On the flip side, federal courts definitely have their own *procedural* rules. The FRCP tells us how long defendants have to respond to lawsuits or how many days they get to file motions. So, you guessed it, federal courts will apply federal rules when deciding procedural issues in diversity jurisdiction cases.

Now comes the hard part. Sometimes it's not clear whether an issue is substantive or "procedural." The Erie doctrine sets out the standard for figuring out whether a rule is "substantive" (and thus state law should apply) or whether a rule is procedural (and thus federal law should apply). I won't spoil the fun for you but here's a couple of overarching principles. If there is a federal statute directly on point, or if one of the FRCP rules is directly on point, then the federal court has to apply that federal rule. But it's sometimes hard to tell if the FRCP is on point or not. And if there is no clear federal rule or statue on point, then courts should consider the "twin aims" of the Erie doctrine. Courts are supposed to discourage forum shopping (where the plaintiff looks around for the most favorable law and files in that jurisdiction) and avoid inequitable administration of the laws. Depending on how much emphasis your professor puts on the Erie doctrine, you will grapple with what these concepts mean in practice.

4. Pleadings

So far, our preview of Civil Procedure has considered whether the court has power over the defendant (personal jurisdiction), whether the court has authority over the type of claim (subject matter jurisdiction), and what law to apply (the Erie doctrine for diversity cases). Our lawsuit is therefore moving forward. The next question is what the paperwork should look like.

The first piece of paper is called a "complaint." The plaintiff does not come to court and make their case orally. Instead, they submit a document—a complaint—at the very beginning of the case where they write down the facts and explain why those facts make the defendant legally responsible. A plaintiff can't just list some statutes or rules and say they are entitled to win. Rather, the complaint must be more detailed and include factual claims that, if true, would entitle the plaintiff to win their case.

The next move belongs to the defendant. Commonly, the defendant will file an "answer." In the answer, the defendant will either admit or deny the allegations. As you can imagine, the defendant usually denies most of the allegations, either by saying they are factually untrue, or by saying that even if the factual claims are true that the defendant has a legal defense that permitted him to take whatever actions he took.

Sometimes, the defendant will hold off on filing an answer. Instead, the defendant will file a "Motion to Dismiss." A defendant can move to dismiss for a whole bunch of reasons. (For instance, the defendant can claim there is no subject matter jurisdiction or personal jurisdiction.)

Although there are a bunch of ways for a defendant to move to dismiss a complaint, your professor will probably spend a lot of time on one in particular: the motion to dismiss for failure to state a claim upon which relief can be granted. This is the so-called Rule

12(b)(6) motion because—no surprise here—it's found in that section of the FRCP.

The gist of a Rule 12(b)(6) motion is that no matter how bad the facts are that the plaintiff raises, there is simply no viable claim that makes the defendant liable. If a defendant files a Rule 12(b)(6) motion, she is basically saying to the court "Even if everything the plaintiff said is true, they still have no valid case, so you have to dismiss the complaint." Here's an example:

Imagine that you and I like to shop at the same store and that we both pull into the parking lot on a rainy day. As I am walking into the store under my umbrella, you are about 20 feet behind me. You have no umbrella, and you are getting absolutely drenched from the rain. You call out to me "Hey, please hold the door for me." Because I'm not a very nice person, I look back at you and say "No. You should learn to plan ahead. Bring an umbrella next time." As the door closes, you have to fumble to open it and a gust of wind knocks you over. You are wet and sore and very mad at me. Indeed, you are so angry that you file a lawsuit against me. Your complaint details all of the facts above. I can respond with a Rule 12(b)(6) motion and say "Even if every fact that you said were true, there is simply no law that requires me to hold the door for you and talk nicely to you." You have failed to state a claim upon which relief can be granted.

One key thing to notice about Rule 12(b)(6) motions is that the facts alleged by the plaintiff have to be assumed to be true. Why is that? Well, a Rule 12(b)(6) motion is filed very early in the life of the case. There has been no discovery yet. No one has quizzed the parties during depositions. And no documents have been produced to either side. So, the court can't possibly know yet whether the plaintiff's factual claims are true. Remember, the defendant is trying to get the case thrown out at the very beginning of the lawsuit. Because we don't know if the plaintiff's factual claims are true and because the defendant is trying to get the case dismissed before we can find out what's true and what's not, we have to assume the plaintiff's allegations are true.

Students struggle with assuming the plaintiff's facts are true, especially when the facts seem one sided. Here's an example: Imagine that you and I are in a car accident. You say that I ran a red light and crashed into you. When I file my Rule 12(b)6) motion to dismiss, I point out that there were five witnesses to the accident and that all five are members of the clergy with impeccable reputations. And all five witnesses say that my light was green, not red. Moreover, the plaintiff has a long history of lying, including multiple theft convictions. Is the lopsided believability of the witnesses a basis to dismiss the plaintiff's case? Absolutely not. Even though a lot of persuasive evidence suggests my light was green, the court must assume at this early stage that the facts are as the plaintiff stated them.

5. Discovery

If the plaintiff has survived the motions to dismiss, we then move on discovery. This is where the plaintiff seeks information to strengthen her case and where the defendant seeks information to tear it down. There are a dozen very detailed rules in the FRCP that govern the discovery process. In many lawsuits, discovery is the whole ball game because discovery flushes out the facts. Once the parties know the core facts and how strong the evidence looks, they are more likely to settle. So it is important for the parties to maximize how much information they can acquire through the discovery process.

Your Civil Procedure course will only scratch the surface of the discovery process, so I'm going to keep it even shorter. Here are the four big discovery tools that parties use most often and that you'll probably learn about:

- Document Requests: Each side can demand that the other side produce relevant documents in their possession or that they control. In the real world, the parties often bitterly fight about whether the other party has complied with its obligations to turn over documents.
- Depositions: Witnesses can be forced to give pre-trial testimony under oath. Even though it's possible to take depositions in writing they are usually done orally, in person, and are transcribed by a court reporter or video-recorded. Each party can depose fact witnesses as well as expert witnesses.
- Interrogatories: The rules permit each party to write out specific questions and to then insist the other party answer those questions.
- Requests for Admission: One party can make a statement and the other party then has to admit or deny whether the statement is true. As a strategic matter, parties will often use Requests for Admission after they have gathered documents and taken depositions. That way, the party will have more information at its disposal before writing its Requests for Admission.

The judge will typically enter a discovery order at the beginning of a case that sets the discovery deadlines. If all goes smoothly, the judge steps back and the parties conduct discovery on their own, working out any disputes by themselves. Here's a shocker though: discovery does not always go smoothly. Parties often fight about what documents have to be produced, the timeliness of scheduling depositions, and the adequacy of responses to interrogatories. Very often, the judge has to get involved. So, let's talk briefly about discovery *disputes*.

If one party thinks the other has not complied with the discovery rules, that party can file a *motion to compel*. This is a motion asking the judge to order a party to turn over evidence or to do something else (such as sit for a deposition). If the judge grants the motion to compel, the resisting party has no choice but to comply.

On the other hand, if a party thinks it is being asked to turn over things it shouldn't have to, that party can file a *motion for a protective order*. That's a motion asking the judge to say something is "off limits." A judge can decide to fully protect documents or information from discovery, or the judge could issue a partial protective order and limit the discovery in some way.

One common discovery fight is about privileged material. Parties do not have to disclose attorney-client privileged communications or "work product doctrine." The attorney-client privilege protects confidential communications between a client and her lawyer. The work product doctrine covers material prepared in anticipation of litigation. For example, if a lawyer wrote herself notes to prepare for the litigation, or if the lawyer's team created charts or graphs to get ready for trial, those would be work product and not discoverable.

Your professor will likely go into considerable detail about the standards for the attorney-client privilege and the work product doctrine. You will grapple with tricky cases in which it is debatable whether those doctrines apply. And you will likely learn in greater detail about the requirements for document requests, depositions, interrogatories, and requests for admission than I have explained above. For now though, you don't have to worry about all those details. Rather, your goal should be to have a very basic understanding of the tools parties use to gather information from their adversary and to protect their own information from disclosure.

6. Joinder

In a basic lawsuit, there is one plaintiff, one defendant, and one claim. For example, remember our hypothetical where I crashed my rental car into your vehicle. You will sue me—and only me—for damage to your car. Pretty simple. But lawsuits can become more complicated. Perhaps I showed up at your house the next day and ran over your mailbox. You might add a second claim. Or perhaps after you file your complaint against me, I decide to add my own claim because you kicked my car after the accident. As you start to consider all the ways a lawsuit can get more complicated, you will have to learn some concepts about additional claims:

- Counterclaims: The defendant can respond to a lawsuit by adding their own claims against the plaintiff. In fact, in some situations, the defendant is *required* to add their counterclaims to the lawsuit so that everything from one event will be litigated together.

- Crossclaims: If the plaintiff sues two defendants (D1 and D2), those defendants can bring crossclaims against each other. D1 can file a "crossclaim" against D2. In our car accident case, imagine that the plaintiff sues both the driver and the rental car company. The driver can file a crossclaim against the rental car company.

In addition to joinder of claims, it is also possible to join *parties*. In other words, just because the lawsuit starts with one plaintiff and one defendant does not mean it will stay that way. Both plaintiffs and defendants can move to add parties. And, kind of shockingly, the rules allow nonparties to add themselves. Here again is a very simplified summary:

- Compulsory Parties: Parties *must* be joined in a lawsuit if their absence would prevent complete relief. This is true even if the plaintiff doesn't want to sue them. Imagine that Alvin sold his house to twin brothers, Barry and Carl. Alvin sues Barry for scamming him out of the house and seeks to get the property back. Even though Alvin blames fast-talking Barry and holds no ill-will toward Carl, Carl is a co-owner of the property and is therefore a necessary party who must be joined.
- Impleading Third Party Defendants: A defendant can join a third party on the ground that the third-party is liable to the defendant. Think about our car accident hypothetical, where you sued me for crashing into you. If I want to argue that the car was defective, I might "implead" the car manufacturer. That way, I can sue the manufacturer for "indemnification," which is a fancy way of saying that the third party should have to reimburse me for whatever I have to pay to the plaintiff. To make things even more complicated, if the defendant joins (impleads) a third-party defendant, that opens the door to the plaintiff asserting claims directly against the third-party defendant. And to make it even more complicated, the third-party defendant can then, in some circumstances, file counterclaims and crossclaims against the other parties. Again, don't worry about these details just yet. Instead, just be aware that your professor is going to discuss these additional parties and analyze who can bring claims against whom.

- Intervention by Third Parties: Believe it or not, someone who isn't part of the lawsuit (nonparties) can actually add themselves to the lawsuit in limited circumstances. The idea here is that the nonparty has some kind of interest that will be impacted by the lawsuit.

As you can imagine, things can become quite confusing when parties start adding claims, counterclaims, crossclaims, new defendants, third-party defendants, and when nonparties start banging on the door asking to be part of a lawsuit that no one invited them to. The best advice is to (A) learn the rules; and (B) create charts or diagrams with arrows that show you how the different parties and claims relate to each other. In the back of your mind, remember the main goal is to resolve as many disputes at one time as possible, but without compromising fairness.

7. Issue and Claim Preclusion

Your Civil Procedure class isn't just about litigating a single case. Sometimes, after a case is over, one of the parties (usually the plaintiff) tries to take another bite at the apple by filing another lawsuit. There are two sets of rules that usually prevent a second bite at the apple: Claim preclusion (which has a Latin name called *res judicata*) and issue preclusion (which has an even scarier name called collateral estoppel).

An important starting point is to think about how litigating the same thing over and over again is inefficient and unfair. If the defendant puts a lot of resources into defending and winning her case, it is very unfair and wasteful to make her do it all over again. Having one bite at the apple encourages the parties to do their best job at briefing and arguing their case, which in turn makes it more likely that the judge or jury will get to the right outcome. The rules are designed to maximize efficiency.

With that background in mind, the first doctrine—claim preclusion—is pretty straightforward. Look for two lawsuits that are pretty much identical. The same plaintiff and the same defendant were in both lawsuits. And the lawsuits were about the same legal claim. Let's do an example.

Imagine that a musician named Adam claims that another artist named Zaria stole a musical riff from him. Adam claims that he was at a jam session with Zaria on July 12th. Adam alleges that he was playing his new song "Minimum Contacts" in front of Zaria, who then said "Wow, that's a great riff. I'm totally going to steal that riff and put it in one of my songs." Adam has filed suit claiming that Zaria's song (which is called "Interpleader") stole the riff from "Minimum Contacts." The case went to the jury, which rejected Adam's claim. The jury found that there had been no jam session on July 12th and thus Zaria could not have heard the line from the Minimum Contacts song and thus couldn't have stolen anything. The lawsuit thus ended in a "final judgment on the merits," rejecting Adam's claim.

Adam cannot bring a second lawsuit claiming that Zaria's "Interpleader" stole a musical riff from Adam's "Minimum Contacts." This is what courts call *res judicata*. The claim has been decided in the first lawsuit, and Adam is precluded from bringing it again.

Issue preclusion is similar to claim preclusion but it focuses on a single issue that has been conclusively resolved. Issue preclusion is not about the whole legal claim brought in the first lawsuit. It's about a single issue that was part of that first lawsuit. Let's go back to Adam and Zaria to explain.

Adam decides to file a new lawsuit. This time, Adam's claim is that Zaria stole yet another musical riff from one of Adam's songs. In this second lawsuit, Adam points to his song "Erie" and says that Zaria also heard that song during the July 12th jam session and that Zaria stole a musical riff from "Erie."

Do you see how Adam is not raising the same "claim" in the second lawsuit? Sure, the second lawsuit involves the same parties. And sure both claims involve stealing music. But the *claims* are different. In the first lawsuit, Adam said that Zaria stole a riff from "Minimum Contacts." The second lawsuit is claiming a stolen riff from an entirely different song called "Erie." The lawsuits have two different claims. So there can't be *claim* preclusion from the first lawsuit to the second.

But there can be *issue* preclusion. Here is why: In the first lawsuit, the jury decided that there had been no July 12th jam session. That issue has been resolved once and for all between Adam and Zaria. The test for issue preclusion is met because the issue of whether there was a jam session was raised in the first lawsuit, it was actually litigated and decided by the jury, and the issue was necessary to the first lawsuit. As such, the jury in the first lawsuit decided—once and for all—that there was no July 12th jam session. Adam cannot come back to court a second time and base his claim on an issue that has already been resolved against him.

Points to Remember

- It is very important that you carefully read each of the Federal Rules of Civil Procedure that your professor assigns.
- Personal jurisdiction is about whether the defendant had enough contacts with the jurisdiction for the court to have power over him.
- Subject matter jurisdiction is about whether the court has jurisdiction over the type of claim. Consider both federal question jurisdiction and diversity jurisdiction.
- In diversity jurisdiction cases, the federal court will use state law for substantive issues and federal law for procedural issues.

- When a defendant moves to dismiss a complaint for failure to state a claim upon which relief can be granted, the court must accept all the plaintiff's factual allegations as true. The question is whether, assuming all those facts are true, the plaintiff has a valid legal claim.
- The discovery process involves document requests, depositions, interrogatories, and requests for admission. Parties may fight discovery by claiming attorney-client privilege, work-product doctrine, and by seeking a protective order.
- Just because a lawsuit starts with one plaintiff, one defendant, and one claim does not mean it will continue that way. The parties can add additional claims, counterclaims and crossclaims. And new parties can be joined by impleading third-party defendants and even by nonparties intervening and adding themselves.
- Once a lawsuit is over, you may have to analyze whether a second lawsuit can be brought. If a party tries to relitigate the same claim, it will typically be barred by claim preclusion. And if a party tries to relitigate a specific issue from the first lawsuit it may be barred by issue preclusion.

CHAPTER 5

Contracts

People enter into millions of contracts every year in the United States. You might think of a contract as a very formal document with lots of legalese and conditions that is signed on the dotted line when you buy something very important, such as a house or a car. But you have surely entered lots of other contracts—for goods and services—without really giving it much thought. Sometimes those contracts are written documents where a vendor dictates the terms that you have no choice but to agree to. Other times you have negotiated the transaction. Some of your agreements were probably well drafted while others weren't. Some of your contracts were airtight, while a handful may not have even been enforceable. Contracts are everywhere in the United States.

Even though people enter into contracts constantly, most of your 1L Contracts class will not teach you how to write airtight contracts. Your professor might do a few drafting exercises to show you how difficult it is to write a tight contract that "thinks of everything." But many 1Ls will not write a single contract in their Contracts class. (Your law school probably has an upper-level drafting course you can take as a 2L or 3L.) Nor will your 1L Contracts class be about negotiating the terms of a contract. So if the 1L Contracts class is not about *writing or negotiating* contracts, what is it about?

Your Contracts class will likely center around the following issues:

1. *Formation*: Has a contract actually been formed? Just because one or both parties think they have made an agreement doesn't mean they actually have done so.

2. *Enforceability*: If an agreement has been formed is it an enforceable agreement, or did something problematic happen that makes the agreement unenforceable?

3. *Terms*: If an agreement has been reached what are the terms of the agreement? Usually, the only terms are what is in the document, right? Not so fast. Sometimes part of an agreement is incomplete or a term isn't defined and we need to look elsewhere to figure out what it means.

4. *Breach*: If there is a valid agreement, has one of the parties breached the agreement? In particular, is any variation from the terms of an agreement—even a tiny one—enough to be a problem? Or is close enough good enough?

5. *Remedy*: If a valid contract has been breached, what is the remedy? Do we order the parties to perform the agreement as written? Or do we give the party that has been wronged "damages" (a fancy word for money)? And if money damages are the right solution, how do we figure out how much the damages should be?

Your Contracts class will surely explore other questions. But these five topics are going to make up a huge part of your Contracts class so let's get into more detail on each of them.

1. Has a Contract Been Formed?

Most 1L Contracts classes focus on legal doctrine and theory. Your professor wants you to understand the nuts and bolts of the legal doctrine that makes up an enforceable contract. So you will spend a lot of time on the unusual cases. Think of it this way: People enter into lots of contracts that are definitely binding contracts. When you sign a lengthy document to buy a car and give the car dealer money in exchange that was definitely a contract. When you sign an apartment lease and promise to pay the rent each month you are signing a binding contract. These are the easy cases, and you won't spend time on them. Instead, you are going to spend a lot of time on the weird cases where one side argues that there really was no agreement. Your professor does that to "build the house from the ground up." They want you to understand the legal concepts that make up a valid contract.

You will start at the very beginning and figure out what an "offer" is. Initially this seems simple. If I write a letter to a lawn mowing service and say "I offer to pay you $40 in exchange for you cutting my grass on Monday" that sure seems like an offer. But things quickly get complicated and uncertain. What if the letter never uses the magic words "I offer"? Or what if the offer seems ludicrous, for instance a professional comedian stops her comedy show and says "I offer to give you the deed to my mansion if you take off your clothes and dance around naked on stage for two minutes?" Or how about if an animal lover makes what seems like a serious offer—"I'll give you $200 to watch my dog while I'm out of town"—but the animal lover was only joking? There are a million hypotheticals like these that you will consider in your Contracts class.

What you'll soon see is that the answers are all guided by two basic principles. First, there are no magic words necessary to create a contract. Second, we don't care what the comedian thought she was doing or if the animal lover believed she was joking. The subjective view of the parties is not relevant. Instead, contract law—like a lot of 1L legal doctrine—is based on what a reasonable person would have understood from the circumstances.

Once you've got a valid offer, you will learn what counts as an "acceptance." Again, things start simple but the questions eventually become complicated. For instance, do you have to say "I accept your offer to pay me for cutting your grass" or can you accept by just showing up at the house and cutting the grass? (Answer: You can usually accept by performing, but not always.) Or consider the even more complicated question of an "acceptance" that changes the terms. For example, is it an acceptance if the lawn company writes back and says "We agree to cut your lawn for $40, but we can only do it on Tuesday." (Answer: This is not usually a valid acceptance, but instead is a counteroffer because it changes the terms.)

The rules for offer an acceptance are important. As are the rules for other contract formation doctrines, such as what to do when the parties totally misunderstood each other and think they are agreeing to the same thing but are actually agreeing to different things. (In the classic case, the parties contracted for cargo on a ship, but there were two ships with the same name and the parties were each talking about a different ship.)

The rules are important, but you should also start to see the bigger picture about why the courts choose the rules. Contract law is not just about resolving the dispute in front of the court, but also about creating rules that will result in smooth transactions for future parties. Courts want to create clear rules that will sit there in the background so that everyone will know the rules when they are negotiating a transaction. When everyone knows the rules of the road, the free market operates faster and with fewer disputes.

2. Is the Contract Enforceable?

Once you've learned about forming a contract, your professor will move on and cover which contracts are enforceable. In reality, most contracts are enforceable. But there's not much legal doctrine or theory for your professor to discuss about run-of-the-mill enforceable contracts. So your textbook and your professor will spend most of the time on the unusual scenarios where the contract is *not* enforceable.

What kinds of unenforceable contracts are you going to cover? A couple of examples include contracts signed by under-age children, contracts signed under duress, contracts where there is a lack of consideration, and unconscionable contracts.

Let's start with the easy one. Normally, children can't enter into contracts. Don't expect to spend much time on kids striking deals.

A harder concept to think through is that a contract can't be valid if it was entered under duress. Obviously, a contract signed with a gun to your head can't be valid. But what if two parties already have a contract, and one party—totally out of the blue—says they will not uphold their end of the deal unless the contract is amended so that they get paid more. If the other party agrees to pay more, it appears they have done so under duress and that the revised agreement is not enforceable.

Another tricky problem is contracts without "consideration." Consideration is a fancy way of saying that each side has to exchange something of value. You can't have a valid contract if one side is giving something valuable and the other side is literally giving nothing in return. One example of this is if someone promises to give you a gift. If they never follow through, you can't claim that they breached a contract with you. You will learn what counts as consideration and how courts respond to completely one-sided contracts.

And then there is the much-debated question of unconscionable contracts. Lots of people enter into deals that turn out to be terrible for them. Those deals are almost always enforceable because each party knew what they were agreeing to and chose freely. Being unhappy or disappointed in your deal does not make it unenforceable.

But sometimes a deal is so convoluted that one of the parties did not really understand what they were getting themselves into. These cases often involve a disparity in bargaining power. So courts will occasionally refuse to enforce some contracts because they were *procedurally* unfair. These cases seem justifiable. But sometimes courts call something procedurally unfair when in fact they really think that the deal was *substantively* unfair. This looks like the court putting its thumb on the scale to help the "little guy." Courts aren't usually supposed to do that in the contracts world, but sometimes they sneak it in. Once again, there is legal doctrine to learn but also bigger-picture questions to grapple with. In particular should courts just be setting out clear rules and getting out of the way, or should courts be evening the playing field to make bargaining fairer? Your professor will probably make you struggle with this question.

3. What Are the Terms of the Deal, and What Do We Do About Unclear Terms?

This topic seems like it should be easy. The contract is whatever is written in the agreement. Nothing more, nothing less, right? That's usually true, but not always. Your professor will introduce you to something called the "parol evidence rule" which has nothing to do with getting out of prison. (That would require an "e" at the end to get you "parole." The word "parol" comes from the French word meaning "verbal."). The parol evidence rule basically says that only the written contract matters and that a party can't show up in court claiming there are additional promises made besides those written on the paper. Once again, your professor will be pushing you to understand not just the rule but the logic behind the rule. So let's do a simple example so that you have some background before you get to more complicated problems.

Imagine you come to my office at the law school and say "Hey, I want to ace the Contracts exam. Can you help me study?" We discuss it for a while and I agree to sell you my class notes in exchange for $50. We write up the deal in which I tell you I will deliver you 200 pages of typed, organized, class notes on Wednesday and you will Venmo me $50. We both sign the document. On Wednesday, I bring you the typed notes. Before accepting the notes and sending me $50 though, you say "Hey, you also promised to make sure I understand the class notes and said you'd answer any follow-up questions I send by email." The promise about answering follow-up questions was not in the written contract. You claim that as I was signing the contract, I orally said that I would answer follow-up questions. I claim to have made no such oral promise. Do I have to answer your follow-up questions? Probably not.

The parol evidence rule says that if a document is "completely integrated"—a fancy phrase for complete—that document has the only terms of the contract. There can be no oral side agreements when a document is completely integrated.

Like the other doctrines you learn, your professor will want you to understand the reasons for the parol evidence rule. And the reasons are straightforward. People discuss lots of things when they are negotiating a contract. Conversations drift from topic to topic and people sometimes mis-hear things or assume things that weren't agreed to. The free market works better if everyone is on the same page. And everyone is more likely to be on the same page if we are all working from the same written terms. Plus, people sometimes lie. A dishonest person trying to save money could promise a smaller amount of money in exchange for one item, but then insist they were also promised a second item orally. If we allowed unclear oral side deals to be enforceable, sellers would start to lose money on their deals. They might stop selling their products. I might stop selling my class notes altogether.[1] Or sellers might increase their prices because of the risk that they're going to be scammed into doing extra work. For example, I might raise the price of my class notes from $50 to $100. In these situations, everyone is worse off. So we need a simple rule—the only terms of the deal are in the ones in the written contract—in order to make the free market work effectively.

So the normal rule is that when we want to know the terms of an agreement we should only look at the written terms. Unfortunately, that does not always work. Sometimes the terms of a contract are ambiguous. The most famous case (which you'll surely read in class) involved a seller's promise to provide "chicken" to the buyer. The seller thought it was allowed to provide cheap chickens for stewing. The buyer thought it was purchasing better-quality chickens for broiling. So the court (and you) have to ask: What does "chicken" mean? Surprisingly, the contract included no definition.

Once again, you should think about not just the case in front of you but of all future parties. Courts and legislatures should want to design rules that make the free market work better and that put

---

1 In case you were wondering, I don't actually sell my class notes. But I do have recommendations for study guides. See Chapter 12.

everyone on the same page. With that in mind, you'll see that courts usually turn first to the "plain meaning" rule and say that terms of a contract are not "ambiguous" if there is a plain meaning for those terms. But what if there is no plain meaning? After all, there's a lot of types of chicken out there! Well, in those cases we will look outside the terms of the contract and consider evidence of what the term should mean under the circumstances. We might turn to expert witnesses or perhaps to the custom in the trade. In the chicken case, we might ask what do chicken sellers and buyers who make similar deals all the time usually understand the term "chicken" to mean?

At the end of the day, your Contracts class isn't about understanding what the word "chicken" means. It's pretty unlikely you're going to spend your career negotiating a lot of contracts about chicken. Instead, it is about understanding the larger issue of *when* it is okay to look outside the written document to understand what the terms of the deal are. It is also about understanding *how* you should figure out what those terms are. And remember that courts are doing this not just to solve the problem for the two parties in the current dispute but also to ensure that future transactions go smoothly.

4. When Has a Contract Been Breached and Is the Breach Material?

In most cases, it is obvious when one party has broken their end of the deal. If I promise to sell you my car on Tuesday but then never show up to deliver the car, then I have broken my promise. In contracts terms, this is called "breaching." Your professor won't spend time on flagrant and obvious breaches. Instead, they will focus on one party failing to comply with the contract in a small way. This raises the question of whether there is such a thing as "close enough" in contract law? Sometimes yes, sometimes no. Let's start with a hypothetical based on a famous case that you will definitely read during your 1L year.

Imagine that a contractor agrees to build a house in exchange for the buyer paying $300,000. The contract has lots of details about how to build the house, including seemingly mundane details such as the type of pipe to use in the plumbing. Let's say that the contract includes a term specifying that the pipe be made by the "Great Piping Company." Just before the house was completely built, the buyer discovered that the contractor had not used the pipe from the Great Piping Company but instead had used pipe from the "Fantastic Piping Company." It turns out that Great Piping and Fantastic Piping are competitors and that they both produce comparably excellent pipe. If you asked a bunch of contractors they would all say, "Those two types of pipe are basically the same." Our buyer doesn't see it that way though. He contracted for "Great Piping" and wants the contractor to put in the pipe that he contracted for. Our contractor really doesn't want to do that though because he has already installed comparable piping. Ripping out the old pipe and installing new pipe would cost a fortune. Our contractor says the piping he installed is "close enough." Or, in contract terms, our contractor says there has been "substantial performance."

Should substantial performance be sufficient? Well, it depends. And this is an area where you can start to see different theories and themes of contract law colliding. On the one hand, contract law favors certainty and the ability for people to negotiate for what they want. If people and companies are crystal clear about what they want, then we should honor that. On the other hand, contract law also favors efficiency. If contractors are worried about being sued for minor variations by sneaky homeowners, they are going to protect themselves by raising prices to cover litigation costs. That's bad for everyone. Notice again how the values we are interested in advancing might shape the rules the court will choose.

Sometimes, courts will allow substantial performance because they will look at the purpose to be served by the contract. In our pipe case, why do you think the contract said "Great Piping Company?" Well, it could be that the homeowner had a real love of Great Piping Company. Perhaps his favorite grandparent had worked at that company. But that seems pretty far-fetched. A more likely explanation is that Great Piping is a good brand of pipe, and the homebuyer was effectively saying:

> "Hey, I am paying you $300,000 for this house, and I don't want you putting crappy plumbing in the walls, so you have to put in good piping. And I don't know how to explain what's good piping as opposed to bad piping, so I'll make that clear by listing the name of a company that makes quality piping."

That's a convincing explanation and the court bought it in the piping case. But courts won't always let parties skate by with substantial performance. For instance, if the contract clearly indicates that "perfect" performance is required and that certain products must be used, courts will often honor that. If in the home contract we've been talking about our buyer said "the contractor must use nothing other than Great Piping because that is the only pipe I trust" then substantial performance would not fly.

5. What Is the Remedy for Breaching a Contract?

As you make your way to the end of your Contracts course, you will have to figure out what to do when someone breaches a contract. We don't just let parties walk away from contracts. The reason—as you've already seen—is that we want people to enter into agreements and feel confident that they can rely on those agreements. Certainty and stability is important to a functioning free market. So we need people to stick by their deals. And the way we get people to stick by their deals is by holding their feet to the fire.

The question though is how to hold someone's feet to the fire. Should we force a breaching party to do exactly what it promised? That is called specific performance. Or should courts instead say to themselves, "Well, maybe there is a good reason not to force the breaching party to do exactly what it promised and instead to just have them pay damages to the other party so that the other party makes the money it expected to make."

Your instinct will probably be that courts should order specific performance because a contract is a contract and people should keep their promises. Surprisingly, courts usually see it the other way and refuse to order parties to do exactly what they promised. And there are good reasons why courts typically go with damages rather than specific performance.

First, sometimes people can't physically keep their promises. If you promised to sell 100 pounds of fruit but your crops were destroyed by a hurricane, you can't deliver fruit because you don't have any.

Second, sometimes it's better for everyone if we don't order specific performance. For instance, imagine that Amy promised to sell Becca 100 pounds of strawberries for $400. But then Carrie came along and offered to pay Amy $500 for those same strawberries because she has a strawberry emergency. Also imagine that if Becca had to buy her strawberries from someone other than Amy that she would end up paying $425 for them on the open market. In terms of overall benefit, it makes sense for Amy to sell the strawberries to Carrie at the higher price and for Amy to then pay $25 in damages to Becca to cover Becca's extra costs. This way, Amy makes a bigger profit, Carrie gets her emergency strawberries, and Becca is not any worse off because the damages covered the higher cost of buying the strawberries from someone else. You'll learn that this is called an "efficient breach" and in the real world companies sometimes do this. Courts don't want to stop parties from making an efficient breach because it's good for the economy. So courts order money damages as the remedy rather than specific performance.

For these reasons, specific performance is pretty rare. It's usually reserved for the sale of unique items that can't be replaced on the open market. For instance, a unique painting or an antique car. So the remedies section of your Contracts course is more likely to focus on how courts should calculate damages.

You will probably cover a bunch of damages concepts in your Contracts class. For example, damages typically have to be foreseeable and capable of being quantified. And the party that is entitled to damages has a duty to mitigate its damages, i.e. to limit how bad the damages will be. You may also learn that there are no emotional or punitive damages in contract disputes. In short, there are a lot of legal rules about damages, and it's hard to predict which topics your particular professor will focus on.

While I can't say exactly what you'll spend your class time on, the key theme is that damages are supposed to make the non-breaching party "whole." In other words, the "victim" should be put back in the same position as if the contract had been carried out exactly as written. The "victim" doesn't get paid *extra* money because the other party breached and behaved badly. Rather, the "victim" should end up in the *same* position, not a *worse* position. For this reason the most common concept you'll encounter is expectation damages—the idea that the victim of the breach should be in the same position as if the contract had been performed exactly as written.

Let's do a quick example so that you'll understand the basic rule before you get to the more complicated stuff in class. Imagine that you booked a rental car with a company called "Cheapest Rentals." The agreement says you will pay $100 to rent the car for the day. However, when you show up at the desk at "Cheapest Car Rentals," they tell you they don't have a car for you to take. That's obviously a breach of the deal.

Maybe the agent admits to breaching for a bad reason and tells you that "a celebrity just came in here 10 minutes before you and we decided to give them your rental car because they are famous." Or maybe the agent has a good reason and explains that "our last car just broke." It turns out that the reason for the breach doesn't matter. Cheapest Car Rentals has breached, and they owe you damages to make you whole.

What are those damages? They are the amount of money you'd have to spend in excess of $100 to get the same car rental from another company. So if you go next door and rent a car from "Second Cheapest Car Rentals" for $137, then you'll be out of pocket $37 more than you had planned on paying, and so Cheapest Car Rentals will owe you $37 in damages. Notice that these are "expectation" damages. If you are paid $37 in damages, you've gotten the benefit of what you expected from your original contract with Cheapest Car Rentals. Notice also that you shouldn't be allowed to walk across the street to "Third Cheapest Car Rentals," pay $197 to rent a car, and expect to collect $97 in damages. That would amount to spending more money than necessary. You are supposed to mitigate your damages. Remember that contract law remedies are designed to make the victim whole, not to punish the breaching party.

6. One Last Thing to Note: Common Law vs. the Uniform Commercial Code (UCC)

I promised that your Contracts class would revolve around 5 key topics (formation, enforceability, terms, breach, and remedies). Let me add one more wrinkle that is worth being aware of as you consider those 5 topics. (Sorry!)

As with your Criminal Law course, you are probably not going to learn the law of Idaho, Iowa, Illinois or any other state. Instead, you will focus on two main types of law: common law and the "UCC."

Contracts class is full of common law rules. As we learned in the Criminal Law chapter, judges have developed legal doctrine over hundreds of years. Common law rules involve judges analyzing precedent and building the next step of legal analysis based on logic and precedent. Most of the legal doctrine you analyze in your Contracts class will be based on common law rules. In other words, when you determine whether something is an "offer" or whether that offer was "accepted" you will turn to prior judicial decisions and logical extension of that precedent.

The other type of law you will focus on is the "UCC" which is short for the "Uniform Commercial Code." In the last century, as businesses and customers increasingly crossed state lines to buy and sell goods, policymakers recognized that it would be challenging to resolve disputes when so many different sets of state laws existed. So, in the 1950s, the American Law Institute (a prominent legal reform group) drafted the UCC—a uniform set of laws that states could adopt that govern various types of commercial transactions. The UCC was very successful. While states haven't all adopted every part of it, the UCC has been widely embraced. The UCC has nine separate parts called "articles." You will not have to worry about most of them. Indeed, you will probably only spend time on Article II of the UCC, which deals with the sale of goods.

The UCC is pretty technical and can be complicated. Some professors delve into a lot of the details. If you're in one of those classes, you should expect lots of discussion of what happens when a transaction goes wrong. For instance, can there be a contract to sell coffee if the agreement doesn't specify the quantity to be sold? What if this is the third such transaction for the sale of coffee between the parties and the previous transactions were all for the same amount of coffee? You will see that the UCC has very specific provisions to answer these kinds of questions.

While some professors think a Contracts class should be filled with UCC discussion, other professors do not. (The split is often between the Contracts professors who study and write scholarly articles about contracts and the "podium" Contracts professors who study and write about a different topic and are teaching the class because the Law School needs them to.) It's probably a little more challenging to be in a class that's heavy on the UCC, but at the end of the day it's not a big deal. The best advice is to follow your professor's lead. If the UCC is important to them, then learn it like you'd learn any other topic in the course. And if the professor doesn't focus on the UCC, then you shouldn't spend a ton of time on it either.

Points to Remember

- The first step is to make sure a contract has been formed. Look for offer, acceptance, and consideration.
- Not all contracts are enforceable though. Sometimes a contract entered under duress or one that is unconscionable will not be enforced.
- Usually, we figure out the terms of the deal by simply reading the contract. This means that one of the parties can't say

"Well, you also orally promised to do other things not in the contract." However, we can sometimes look beyond the written contract, especially if the terms are ambiguous and you need to figure out what they mean.

- Not all breaches of contracts are "material." Sometimes, the doctrine of substantial performance means that "close enough is good enough."
- The remedy for a breach of a contract is rarely specific performance. Courts usually award damages to make the victim whole. Damages ensure that the victim gets what they expected to earn from the transaction. Damages are not designed to punish the breaching party.
- There are two key sets of legal rules you will encounter in your Contracts class. Common law rules are made by judges and typically cover service contracts where one party promises to do something in exchange for payment. The UCC usually covers contracts for the sale of goods.
- Understanding the common law and UCC rules is not the only important part of your Contracts class. You should also think hard about the reasons why the rules are chosen. Courts and legislatures want to encourage contracting. They do this by creating certainty and clarity. Courts also favor rules that enhance efficiency and improve the functioning of the free market.
- To create certainty and clarity, most of contract law focuses on what a reasonable person would think under the circumstances, not what one of the contracting parties subjectively believed.

CHAPTER 6

Constitutional Law

Constitutional Law—"Con Law" as the cool kids call it—is the class students are usually most excited about.[1] You have probably read about the Supreme Court issuing rulings about free speech, religious liberty, privacy, affirmative action, and abortion rights, to name just a few. Your Con Law professor will likely cover some of these controversial topics, so buckle up. Before you get there though, your professor will spend a lot of time on some issues you've probably never thought about, including something called the Commerce Clause, Congress's taxing power, and the question of whether the Constitution even gives courts the power of judicial review in the first place. In short, Con Law is a mix of mundane doctrines and hot-button issues.

Con Law is a different animal than your other 1L courses, so before we get to the specifics, it's important to take a step back and think about what the point of the course is and how you should think about what you're learning.

---

[1] Most law schools cover Con Law in the 1L year, but not all. If your school leaves Con Law until later, then skip this chapter unless you're just really interested in the topic.

The first thing to recognize is that the Constitution is actually really short. The copy I keep in my office is only a dozen pages long, and that's with large font. Why do I tell you that the Constitution is really short? It's to disabuse you of what you've heard in dorm room arguments, family throwdowns at Thanksgiving, and from cable news pundits. When someone says "That politician (who I don't like) is ignoring the Constitution," or "That person is trampling the Constitution!" it's a pretty good bet that they've probably never even read the Constitution. The founders were writing a framework to govern future generations. They weren't writing a tax code with thousands of tiny details. The simple fact is this—the Constitution is really short, so there's not a lot of clear rules written in there.

The second thing to understand (which is definitely related to the document being short) is that most of the Constitution's provisions are open-ended and often unclear. Sure, there are things in the Constitution that are very specific—you have to be 35 years old to be president. But more often, the phrases are murky. The President has to "faithfully" execute the law. Congress can make laws that are "necessary and proper." Everyone is guaranteed "due process" and "equal protection of the laws." What do these things mean? Unlike this book (see Chapter 16!), the Constitution does not have a glossary that lists definitions. The Constitution does not define its terms.

The third thing to see (which is related to the two points above) is that the meaning of open-ended terms in the Constitution is developed over time by the courts, particularly the U.S. Supreme Court. And the development of Con Law can take time and encounter twists and turns along the way. Plus, some important provisions of the Constitution don't give rise to lots of cases. There are millions of land transactions, torts, and crimes every year in the United States, but fewer cases about the legitimacy of Congress's spending power. So Con Law often develops slowly, sometimes changes, and leaves lots of questions unresolved.

Let's put these three background points together. (1) The Constitution is a short document that doesn't have a lot of specific rules in it; (2) most of the "rules" are really just open-ended standards and terms without clear definitions; and (3) courts develop the meaning of the terms and standards slowly over time and those meanings can change. Those three realities mean that your Con Law professor is regularly going to tell you "the answer isn't entirely clear" and "it depends."

That lack of clear answers doesn't mean your professor won't focus on legal doctrine. To the contrary, your professor is definitely going to expect you to know the current state of the law, the tests to use, and where they came from. But the lack of clear answers to many questions and the slow development of the law over time is going to lead your professor to put a lot of emphasis on you making arguments from the principles you've learned. Your professor will come up with scenarios (in class and on the exam) that look nothing like the cases you've read. You'll then have to take the legal doctrine and apply it to these new scenarios. You will certainly do this in your other 1L classes as well, but in Con Law you should expect even fewer clear answers and an even greater focus on your ability to make arguments.

The fourth background principle to know about Con Law is that the dissenting opinions matter a lot. You will read a few dissents in your other 1L courses, but not many. In Con Law, you will read a lot of dissents. If the dissents aren't the law (just the opinion of the justices who lost) why do we care about them? As one of my Con Law colleagues likes to say "Today's dissent may be tomorrow's majority opinion." The dissents showcase flashpoints in the law and provide tea leaves for the arguments in future cases. Read the dissents carefully.

The fifth piece of important background information is that theories of interpretation matter a lot in Con Law. Believe it or not, there are theories about contract interpretation. And there are theories about what constitutes "property." Professors write a lot of books and articles on topics like these. But most students will never read them because courts don't generally pay much attention to interpretive theory. But Con Law is different.

There is a lot of disagreement about *how* to interpret the Constitution. Some judges and scholars think the only relevant inquiry is what the text says. Other judges focus on what the words in the Constitution originally meant when they were written. (This "original meaning" approach requires looking in old dictionaries and treatises.) Still other judges take a more pragmatic view and focus on what the practical outcome of a decision will be. Your professor may draw your attention to the modes of interpreting the Constitution. These theories may seem tangential to you, but they matter because they are often just under the surface of the decisions you will read.

Now that we have some background about the Constitution and what your professor will be trying to accomplish, let's talk about some of the legal doctrine you are going to encounter. Your professor is probably going to talk about four big baskets of Con Law concepts:

1. Judicial Review: Do courts have the power to review federal and state laws and find them unconstitutional?

2. Federalism: What is the balance of power between the federal government and the states?

3. Separation of Powers: What happens when the president wants to do something and Congress or the courts disagree?

4. Rights: Do people have certain rights that prevent the government from adopting laws that conflict with those rights?

1. Judicial Review

Your Con Law course is probably going to start with a guy riding around on a horse in the year 1801. The backstory is that after President John Adams lost re-election in 1800, he nominated some political buddies for judgeships and the Senate confirmed them just before he left office. The only step left was for a formal piece of paper—called a "commission"—to be delivered to each new judge. But there was no FedEx or UPS in 1801, and delivery by horse was kind of slow. So not all of the commissions were delivered before President Adams's term ended. When Thomas Jefferson became president, he wasn't too excited about people from John Adams's political party becoming federal judges at the eleventh hour of the Adams' administration, so he ordered that the commissions not be delivered. Now there was a dispute: The Senate had approved the judgeships, and the new president was refusing to deliver them. Could he do that? And do the courts have the power to review that decision?

If you want to take a moment to search an online copy of the Constitution, I'll wait while you try to figure it out. . . . Are you flummoxed yet? What if you use Control-F and search for "judicial review?" After all, when there is a dispute between the Senate and the President, that seems like a job for the courts, right? Prepare to be disappointed, or at least confused.

You can look all you want, but you won't find the words "judicial review" anywhere in the Constitution. There is nothing anywhere in the document that says courts get to review the constitutionality of laws or presidential actions. That should seem strange to you. After all, it's obvious today that the Supreme Court gets to rule on the constitutionality of federal legislation and presidential actions. But it wasn't obvious back when people were delivering commissions by horseback. The Supreme Court's famous 1803 decision in *Marbury v. Madison* cemented the concept of judicial review.

I won't go over all the details of the *Marbury* decision. Your professor will help you pick apart the case. But suffice it to say, the Supreme Court battled for turf to ensure the power of judicial review over congressional and presidential actions.

Now that judicial review is part of the fabric of American democracy, what is left to study about it? One major challenge that continues to this day is something called the counter-majoritarian difficulty. Your professor will likely bring up this problem as you grapple with the scope of the Supreme Court's authority. Here's a really short synopsis of the problem:

We elect our representatives in Congress. And we elect the President. But we definitely don't elect the Justices on the Supreme Court (or any federal judge for that matter). The only way we have any say over who becomes a federal judge is indirectly, because they are nominated by the President and confirmed by the Senate. And sometimes, those un-elected judges strike down laws that have been enacted by the people's representatives. When the Supreme Court Justices overturn laws enacted by our representatives, the justices are acting "counter" to the will of the "majority," hence the term "counter-majoritarian."

The phrase you'll hear in your Con Law class is counter-majoritarian *difficulty*. We use the word "difficulty" because having justices reject the will of the people can be a good thing in some cases and a bad thing in other instances. Figuring out when judges should be blocking popular will is a "difficult" question. Here's two ways to think about judges rejecting majority will:

On the one hand, no one has elected the Supreme Court Justices to anything. Worse yet, the Constitution says they get to hold their job for life unless they decide to retire. Some of the justices hold onto their jobs until they take their very last breath on this Earth. Even the justices who retire don't usually leave in their early 60s to go sit on a beach. Justices often stay on the court for more than a quarter of a century. Two justices—Oliver Wendell Holmes and John Paul Stevens—stayed on the Court even after they turned 90 years old.[2] Can you imagine that people in their 80s and 90s who have worked in a marble palace[3] for 30 years and been surrounded by a security detail might be a little out of touch? And might they unwisely thwart the will of the majority and interpret the Constitution to strike down a law that should have remained on the books?

On the other hand, sometimes the will of the majority is a bad thing. American history is full of examples of the majority doing terrible things to the minority. The majority sometimes seeks to unfairly take away civil liberties from minority groups based on their religion, race, sexual orientation, or for some other unfair reason. So having life-tenured judges with the power to stop the majority from abusing their power is very important sometimes.

The problem, of course, is that it is not always clear whether the Court is acting in the "good" counter-majoritarian way or the "bad" counter-majoritarian way. You will struggle with this challenge throughout your Con Law course.

2. Federalism

Federalism is about the balance of power between the federal government and the states. Another way to think about how the

---

[2] If you're looking for the secret to living a long life, getting a job as a Supreme Court Justice might just be it.

[3] Maybe "palace" is an exaggeration, but not by much.

Constitution has structured American government is to think about where the power of Congress ends and where the power of the states begins.

Congress has specific powers—the power to regulate commerce; the power to tax, the power to spend, and the power to declare war. You'll hear your professor say those powers are "enumerated," meaning that Congress gets to do those things because they are expressly stated in the Constitution. The flip side of that is that Congress can't exercise powers that are not listed in the Constitution.

If Congress can't do certain things, then who gets to do them? The answer is the states. The Tenth Amendment in the U.S. Constitution specifically says that "the powers not delegated to the United States by the Constitution, nor prohibited by it to the states, are reserved to the states respectively, or to the people."

Initially at least, the concept of limited congressional powers seems simple in principle. Congress can make laws and take actions if the power is listed in the Constitution, but otherwise the states have the power. The reality, of course, is that things are much more complicated than they seem.

For example, the Constitution says that Congress has power to regulate commerce among the several states. But what does that mean? If I build a professional kitchen in Virginia to make and ship my world-famous chocolate-chip cookies to Maryland, Minnesota, and Mississippi, it seems pretty obvious that I'm engaged in commerce among the several states. So Congress can pass laws that regulate the food safety of my professional kitchen and others like it.

But what if I grow my own ingredients for the cookies in my backyard. And what if I only sell my cookies in Virginia? Could that be commerce among the several states because my cookie sales are part of the cookie market generally? After all, when someone loves my local Virginia cookies, they will stop buying Chips Ahoy cookies that are made elsewhere and shipped in interstate commerce to Virginia. So even if my cookies don't leave Virginia, they *affect* interstate commerce.

It might not surprise you to learn that the Court's view of interstate commerce has changed over time. In part, this is because our country has shifted from an agrarian farming society to one that is much more industrial and inter-connected. Additionally, national politics have shifted and membership on the Supreme Court has changed as well. So around the time of the New Deal (when the country was in a more nationalist mood) the Court interpreted the Commerce Clause very expansively, which in turn meant that states' power under the Tenth Amendment diminished. Pretty much everything became interstate commerce.

As the Supreme Court became more conservative on federalism issues in the 1990s, the Court dialed back the scope of the Commerce Clause. Today, Congress continues to have very broad power under the Commerce Clause, but not as broad as in the past. So, Congress can regulate how things move in interstate commerce (think of the roads and the airports) as well as anything that has a "substantial relation" to interstate commerce. But they cannot call non-economic activity interstate commerce just so that they can regulate it.

3. Separation of Powers

As you learned in grade school, there are three branches of government—executive, legislative, and judicial. What you probably didn't realize is that those branches correspond to articles in the Constitution. Article I talks about the legislative branch (Congress); Article II focuses on the executive (the President); and Article III is about the judiciary (the federal courts, and primarily the U.S. Supreme Court).

The idea of separation of powers is to prevent any branch from becoming too powerful. There are checks and balances, with each branch checking the other. For instance, federal judges cannot be appointed by the President without approval of the Senate. Once in their positions, judges can strike down legislation passed by Congress as unconstitutional. And if Congress is very unhappy with a federal judge, the House of Representatives and the Senate (at least theoretically) can work together to remove a judge from office.[4]

In modern America, the heart of the separation of powers doctrine is about the power of the President. For that reason, every Con Law student reads a case called *Youngstown Sheet & Tube Co. v. Sawyer* that the Supreme Court decided during the Korean War. In that case, steelworkers were about to go on strike, which was a big problem because the American army needed steel for the war. So, President Truman issued an executive order to take possession of the steel mills to keep them running. Did the President have that power?

Well, Article II of the Constitution gives the President power as commander-in-chief of the military. But it doesn't say anything about the president having power to nationalize private businesses. Moreover, Congress had never passed legislation granting that power to the President. On the other hand, Congress also hadn't passed legislation telling the President that he couldn't nationalize the steel mills.

There were seven separate opinions in the *Youngstown* case, which is quite a feat given that there are only nine Supreme Court justices. Perhaps more unusual, the majority opinion is not the one

---

4 In reality, this almost never happens.

that 1Ls study in depth. Instead, the concurring opinion of Justice Jackson has become standard reading because it does the best job of explaining how the Court should proceed in separation of powers disputes. Justice Jackson broke the analysis down into three scenarios:

1. The President has the most executive power when she can rely on authority granted by Congress. So if there is a law that expressly (or even implicitly) gives the President power, the President is going to be on the most solid footing.

2. If Congress hasn't spoken on the issue at all—there is no legislation that grants power or forbids it—the President is then in the "zone of twilight" and the President only gets to act if the power is specifically provided in Article II of the Constitution (the article dealing with presidential powers), or if the circumstances around the use of the power make the action "imperative."

3. If Congress has passed a law indicating that a President should *not* do something, then the President has the least power and can only take the action if Congress's law is unconstitutional.

President Truman's actions fell into Category 2—the "zone of twilight." And the Supreme Court decided that he had exceeded the power Article II granted him. The reason is that Article II gives the President the authority to act as commander-in-chief. That doesn't mean he can control everything that is in any way related to the military. After all, the Constitution grants Congress the power to declare war. Beyond that, the Constitution says that Congress has the power to raise and support an Army and a Navy. It looked to the Court like steel production fell closer to *supporting* an army than *commanding* one. So the Court concluded in this "zone of twilight" that the President had overreached into territory that belonged to Congress.

One other interesting thing about the *Youngstown* case is that it is a good example of the Supreme Court throwing its weight around to assert its place in the separation of powers analysis. In limiting the power of the President, the Court preserved its own power by re-asserting its role as the final arbiter of constitutional disputes.

The *Youngstown* opinion is an example of the type of separation of powers disputes you will grapple with. As you explore other cases, you will utilize the *Youngstown* framework. As with other areas of law, however, you'll see that simply having a slogan ("checks and balances!") or even a three-part test does not always offer clear answers.

4. Rights

Many of you came to law school to learn about individual rights and how to protect them. So, this is what you have been waiting for. Your 1L Con Law course is kind of like the appetizer course of a meal though. Don't expect to spend your whole semester on Equality, Due Process, Freedom of Speech, Free Exercise of Religion, and other rights. Odds are that your professor will only cover some of these topics and won't come to them until later in the course. As a 2L or 3L, you will have the opportunity to study all of those topics in more depth, not to mention criminal procedure classes about your search and seizure rights and the right to remain silent. So you should expect your Con Law class to be an introduction to the core concepts, not enough to become an expert. With that in mind, let's dig in just a little bit.

a. *State Action*

The first step in any question of constitutional rights is whether we are talking about "state action." You and I have constitutional rights against the government. We don't have constitutional rights against random people on the street. So if you come to my house and decide you'd like to give a speech in my backyard, I don't have to let you. You have no First Amendment right to speak in private places. The Government can't shut down your free speech rights, but I surely can prevent you from speaking at my house. The state action doctrine raises a key point that people often fail to appreciate: Just because something bad happened to you does not mean that it has violated your constitutional rights. There has to be state action. To bring this point home, consider this simple but disheartening example:

Imagine that the CEO of Initech Company[5] decides to host a poker game at his house. He invites a few of his male employees—Peter, Samir, Michael, Milton, and Tom. This is an opportunity for the employees to hang out with the boss who decides whether or not they get a raise. The CEO doesn't invite a single one of his female or transgender employees to the poker game. When some of those employees who've been excluded hear about the poker party they specifically ask the CEO to attend and he says "Nope, this party is just for men." This is pretty awful behavior by the CEO. He's clearly giving preferential treatment to the male employees. But has the CEO acted unconstitutionally? Nope. Initech is not a state actor, nor is its CEO. Initech and its CEO are private actors. So they can't act unconstitutionally.

Now you might be thinking to yourself that "the CEO must have violated some law" by excluding people based on gender." That's entirely possible. Congress has created lots of employment laws to

---

[5] If you don't get this reference, you should see the movie Office Space.

prevent discrimination on the basis of sex, race, age, disability, and other characteristics. But those are federal *statutes*, they are not *constitutional* law. Your Con Law class is not about employment law. It's about how the provisions of the Constitution restrict the government, not private parties.

So you should always be looking first for state action. If you can point to state action, the next question is whether one of your constitutional rights has been violated. As noted, your Con Law professor is not going to cover all, or even most of, the constitutional provisions. The two big ones you're most likely to focus on are Equal Protection and Due Process.

b. Equal Protection

Like so many other things in your 1L year, "Equal Protection" initially sounds pretty simple. Everyone has to be treated equally, right? But that can't be correct. The government draws distinctions between people all the time. Not everyone gets to drive a car. You have to be old enough and you have to pass a driver's test showing you know the rules of the road. The Supreme Court justices get hundreds of applications for law clerk positions and they throw away most of them (including mine!) And that must be right too. Surely the justices get to pick the law students with the highest grades to be their clerks. The justices are discriminating based on grades. And when the state says you have to be 16 to drive, it is discriminating based on age. But both of those types of discrimination are permissible because the state actors can point to acceptable reasons.

How good do the reasons have to be though? The Court has adopted a tiered approach. Discrimination based on race seems the most indefensible. America has a terrible history of racial discrimination. Eventually, our society came to the conclusion that it's almost impossible to think of a reason why it would be acceptable to treat people worse on account of their race. So the Court has adopted the toughest test—strict scrutiny—for racial discrimination claims. A law that discriminates based on race is only acceptable if the government can point to a compelling justification and that the rule is narrowly tailored to the situation. In these cases, the government almost always loses.

Gender discrimination is subjected to intermediate scrutiny, which is a tough standard, but not as tough as strict scrutiny. The government doesn't need to demonstrate a compelling justification, just an "important" one. And the government need not show a narrowly tailored law, just one that is "substantially related" to the government's purpose. The government often loses under intermediate scrutiny, but not always.

Finally, the third tier of scrutiny is rational basis review. Most other categories (besides race and gender) are analyzed under this low standard of review. The courts will uphold laws as long as they are rationally related to a legitimate purpose. Not surprisingly, the government usually doesn't pass laws with no legitimate purpose. So the government almost always wins equal protection cases under the rational basis test unless it seems like there is a vulnerable group being targeted by the law.

Your task is not simply to remember the levels of scrutiny and which types of discrimination go with each. That is not legal analysis; it is just memorization. Instead, your professor is going to expect you to be able to apply the different levels of scrutiny to situations you have never seen before. For example, the Supreme Court applies strict scrutiny to race and intermediate scrutiny to gender discrimination. But what about sexual orientation?

The other thing to recognize is that the explanation above is not a complete description of the complicated world of Equal Protection analysis. For instance, the Court has held that discriminatory impact—cases where the state did not *intend* to discriminate, but that the *effect* of a law was worse for one group than another—is not enough for an Equal Protection violation. As you'll see, there is a lot of complexity to the law. For now though, you should begin to think about how simple slogans like "everyone is treated equally" don't represent the complex legal analysis you'll have to do.

c. Due Process

There are two Due Process clauses in the Constitution. The Due Process Clause in the 5th Amendment binds the federal government, and a similar clause in the 14th Amendment that was added after the Civil War applies to the states. Both clauses say, in slightly different language that no one should be "deprived of life, liberty, or property, without due process of law." You won't spend your time focusing on the tiny wording variations between the two due process clauses. Instead, you are going to focus on two very different ways in which the due process clauses are relevant: (1) procedural due process and (2) the far more controversial topic of substantive due process. Let's start with the less heated topic.

To understand "procedural due process" you have to focus on the first word: "procedural." It guarantees procedural protection before a person can lose their life, liberty or property. This is easiest to understand in the criminal context. When the government charges a person with murder (which carries a possible sentence of death or life in prison), the government is trying to take away either their life or their liberty. As we all know, the defendant gets some procedural protections before that can happen. And the court needs to follow those procedures.[6] Otherwise, the defendant will have been deprived of procedural due process. So procedural due process

[6] The concept works the same way outside of the criminal arena. If your state university (remember, we need a state actor) wants to expel you for a disciplinary violation, they need to have adequate procedures in place and they need to follow them.

includes procedures like cross-examining witnesses and the option for the defendant to testify. You will probably not spend much time on procedural due process in your Con Law class.

The bigger due process issue in Con Law is *substantive* due process. This is the idea that due process protects some substantive rights because they are so central to freedom that they count as the word "liberty." Substantive due process means that the individual has some right—e.g. the right to privacy—that the state cannot just take away because they first gave you a hearing and an opportunity to make your case. Rather, substantive due process means that you have fundamental rights that are protected against government encroachment.

Right off the bat, you can see why substantive due process is controversial. Critics say that the Supreme Court Justices act as legislators, not judges, when they recognize substantive due process rights that are not specifically mentioned in the Constitution. And critics say that the Justices are using an amorphous term—"due process"—to create rights and treat them the same as the rights that are actually listed in the Constitution and the Bill of Rights. Moreover, some famous constitutional scholars have pointed out that the term "substantive due process" is actually an oxymoron like "deafening silence" or "old news." Substance and process are two words that mean the exact opposite thing. So the idea of saying a constitutional clause focused on "process" is supposed to offer people a substantive legal protection seems backwards.

On the other hand, consider why the 14th Amendment—which contains one of the Due Process clauses—was enacted in the first place. The Civil War was fought to end slavery—the ultimate limitation on freedom. The 14th Amendment came on the heels of the Civil War and the Amendment was created to protect people who could be harmed by government policies. Moreover, another argument for substantive due process comes from how short the

Constitution is. James Madison and friends wrote the Constitution over 230 years ago, and they could not possibly have thought of everything. And some rights that they couldn't or didn't think about in 1787 seem fundamental today.

Your professor will probably engage with your class over the *idea* of substantive due process. You will focus on whether it is legitimate for the Court to be finding substantive due process guarantees. You will then explore the question of *how* the Court should decide which rights are fundamental and protected and which aren't. Along the way, you'll also probably explore the history of substantive due process.

Although today we focus on privacy rights and abortion, the first fight over substantive due process was originally a fight over freedom of contract. Over a hundred years ago, in a famous case called *Lochner v. New York*, the Supreme Court struck down a law that set a maximum number of hours for bakery employees. Today, courts regularly uphold maximum hour laws, but in 1905 the Court held that such laws violated the Due Process Clause. Although the *Lochner* decision never used the phrase "substantive due process," the concept was identical. Legislatures were not allowed to restrict the freedom of contract because people had a fundamental right to contract. If you wanted to work 100 hours a week as a baker, the Constitution protected that right.

As you'll learn, *Lochner* has long since been overruled. But the history is relevant to thinking about the Court's role in assessing the constitutionality of legislation that restricts liberty. The other historical precedent you'll surely read is *Griswold v. Connecticut*, a case about the right to contraception. The *Griswold* decision is the foundational case creating a constitutional right to privacy, though the Court wasn't entirely clear about what constitutional provision guaranteed that right.

All of this will lead up to the abortion decisions, one of the biggest fights in the history of constitutional law. Your professor will cover the creation of the right to abortion in *Roe v. Wade*, the Court's decisions chipping away of that right over the next four decades, and then ultimately the *Dobbs* decision, which overruled *Roe* and eliminated the substantive due process right to abortion. This is challenging material, both in terms of the legal concepts and people's strong feelings about the Court's decisions.

As you discuss the Court's abortion decisions, you will be reminded of many of the themes that cut across your entire Con Law class. The Constitution is short and doesn't answer all of the questions. So judges are asked to step in and fill gaps. This highlights the counter-majoritarian difficulty. And it raises not just the question of when courts should insert themselves, but also *how* they should approach decisionmaking. Should courts be guided by the text of the Constitution alone? Should they focus on the original understanding of the Constitution at the time it was adopted? Should courts turn to history, but only as a general guide? Or should judges see their job as pragmatists who should be concerned with ensuring just outcomes and maximizing liberty? As you go through your semester of Con Law, try to remind yourself of all these questions.

Points To Remember

- The Constitution is really short. It doesn't list a lot of specific rules and it leaves a lot of questions unanswered.
- Your Con Law class will partly be about learning doctrine, but much more so about learning how to make arguments in unclear circumstances.
- Read the dissents. Today's dissent may be tomorrow's majority.
- Judicial review isn't stated in the Constitution, but it has become a crucial part of American democracy.

- The counter-majoritarian difficulty is a constant problem in Con Law. Unelected judges can unwisely thwart the will of the people. On the other hand, sometimes the majority tries to oppress the minority and the judiciary is what prevents tyranny of the majority.
- Federalism is the balance of power between the federal government and the states.
- Congress has enumerated powers to tax, spend, declare war, regulate commerce among the several states, and a couple of other less prominent powers. Other powers not enumerated in the Constitution belong to the states.
- In modern America, the doctrine of separation of powers is really a question about the scope of presidential power.
- The Constitution restricts the actions of state actors. We have constitutional rights against the government, not against private actors. The government can't take away your free speech rights, but you have no free speech rights in my backyard.
- Equal Protection doctrine is more complicated than simply "everyone should be treated the same." The Supreme Court has created three different levels of scrutiny—strict, intermediate, and rational basis—depending on the type of alleged discrimination.
- The Constitution's guarantee of due process falls into two categories: procedural due process and substantive due process.
- Procedural due process requires certain procedural safeguards before the government can take away life, liberty, or property.

- Substantive due process provides that certain liberties are fundamental and cannot be taken away by the government.

CHAPTER 7

Property

For most students, Property is the hardest 1L class. There are a few reasons. First, there are a ton of rules to learn in your Property class. Second, a lot of those rules include complex terms that kind of sound the same but actually have very different meanings. Third, there often isn't a piece of paper that clearly says who owns what property and explains what they are allowed to do with it. Finally, there are underlying theories of property law that drive the outcome of the cases, and unfortunately sometimes those theories conflict with each other. The good news is that while Property is challenging, it is fascinating to explore who really owns what. Before we jump into the subjects you'll cover in Property, let's start by explaining some Property theory.

1. Property Theory That Courts and Professors Like to Use

1. <u>Bundle of Sticks</u>: Professors love to talk about property as a bundle of sticks.[1] The idea is that property isn't just one right, but a bunch of rights.

---

[1] Maybe it's because none of them are outdoorsy enough to build a fire.

Imagine that you buy an acre of land with a small house on it. Think of all the things you could do with that land.

You could *sell* the entire land and the house to me! Or you could *divide* the land in half and sell the part with the house to me and the empty half to someone else so that they can build another house. You could go in a different direction and *improve* the property by building a swimming pool in back of the house. Or you could *exclude* others, by refusing to let your siblings come to visit.

Each one of these rights—dividing, selling, improving, or excluding—is a stick in your bundle of property rights. Your professor will get you to think about each of these property interests and others as well.

2. Property Law Favors Productive Use of the Land: One of the first rude awakenings for law students is that even though you own a piece of property, other people can sometimes use your land or limit what you can do with it. For instance, if your neighbor is landlocked and can't get to the road, they may be able to get an "easement" to walk or drive across your property. Or imagine that you own a tract of land and you just ignore it for a decade. During that time, someone might build a house on *your* land. When you later tell them to get out, you'll discover that *they* now own it through something called "adverse possession." The reason is that the law favors productive use of the land. It is better for land to be used than for it to sit idle.

3. <u>The Least Cost Avoider</u>: Property law is often viewed through a lens called "Law and Economics." This is the idea that economic principles can help us to come up with the most effective and efficient set of legal rules. One economic principle you'll see is the "least costs avoider," which is the idea that the losing party is the one who could have most easily avoided the problem. For example, let's say that there is a piece of property next to a garbage dump. I buy the property and want to build a house on it, but the smell from the dump is so terrible that no one could stand to live there while the garbage dump is operating. I am the "least cost avoider." It would be much easier for me to pick a different piece of property than it would be for the garbage dump to get rid of the smell. So the garbage dump wins in our dispute.

4. <u>Honoring Reasonable Expectations</u>: Just because there is a more efficient way to decide a property dispute between two parties does not mean that efficiency always wins. Imagine three homes on a quiet street that is next to a huge 50-acre tract of undeveloped land. A corporation buys the undeveloped land hoping to turn it into a giant, smoky factory. In this case, a court is probably going to honor the reasonable expectations that the homeowners had when they bought their houses and prevent the corporation from building the factory.

Our last example shows the challenges you will face in thinking about property law. The three homeowners have reasonable expectations that the neighboring property will be for residential homes, not factories. But notice that no one has built houses there.

Surely having a factory that manufactures something is a more productive use of the land than having it sit empty. Moreover, the three homeowners could move elsewhere without too much trouble, whereas it's hard to find an undeveloped plot of land large enough to build a huge factory. The homeowners seem like the least cost avoider. Notice that the underlying theories that explain property law conflict in this case. If you see the conflict, you are well on your way to understanding how to think about property law.

2. Topics in Your Property Class

Now that we have some background on property theory, let's talk about the topics you will study in your Property class. Spoiler alert: there are a lot of topics. In some law schools, Property is actually more credits than the other 1L classes. And in other law schools, professors jam a ton of material into the same number of credits. Because some Property classes are overflowing with content, this chapter is a little longer than the chapters about the other 1L classes. Your professor may not cover all of these topics. But odds are, these are the main topics you are likely to see:

1. <u>Estates and Future Interests</u> focus on what you actually own and what you can do with it in the future. For instance, if you sell me a house in "fee simple," that means it's entirely mine. I can do whatever I want with it, and I can sell or give it to whoever I want. But if someone gives me a "life estate" for that same house, that means it belongs to me while I'm living, but that after I die it goes back to the person who gave it to me or someone else they choose. My life estate gives me less control over the property. I can't destroy it, and I can't sell it. There are other much more complicated types of

ownership interests besides fee simple and life estates, so buckle up.

2. Concurrent Estates: More than one person can own the same piece of property. Think of a married couple, or perhaps two families that co-own a beach house. The three main ways to co-own property are Joint Tenancy, Tenancy by the Entirety, and Tenancy in Common. The differences are quite important but not that complicated, so I'll save that explanation for later in this chapter.

3. Landlord Tenant Law: When you sign a lease to rent an apartment, there is usually a long contract that sets out your rights and the landlord's rights. Most of the rules are covered by contract law. But states often impose additional landlord-tenant rules to ensure that residential tenants don't get completely railroaded. Your Property class may cover some of the basic landlord-tenant rules imposed by state property law.

4. Servitudes are non-possessory interests in land. That probably sounds complicated. For now, let's ease into the concept by thinking about the simplest non-possessory interest—an easement. Imagine that I own a house on a gorgeous beach. My neighbor can't get to the beach from her lot, so I sell her a right to walk across my land to get to the beach. The neighbor's right to walk across my property is an affirmative easement. You'll learn that property law also recognizes something called negative easements. For instance, my neighbor might have the ability to prevent me from building a five-story

house on my lot that prevents her from seeing the ocean.

5. Land Transactions: There is more to selling a house than simply writing a contract that says "Betty sells 123 Main Street to Adam." The reason for the additional rules is that the government wants to avoid disputes that result from confusing circumstances or bad actors. For example, what if Betty signs a contract to sell the property to me and then signs a separate contract to sell the same property to Carla? Now who owns the property? To avoid these problems, property law has rules about recording deeds to property. The deed passes title from one person to another. The buyer then "records" the deed with the government so that it will be on file for the whole world to know about. All of this seems simple at first, but things can be much more complicated. It turns out that there are different kinds of deeds that offer different levels of protection. And states have different types of recording rules that you will also learn about.

6. Zoning: Think about the city or town where you grew up.[2] Odds are that there aren't houses built next to gas stations. The reason is that the city planners design areas of the city for people to live in (residential) and areas for businesses (commercial), as well as mixed-use zones in between. This is called zoning. But with every zoning plan comes exceptions, so your professor will teach you not only about the different types of zones but also about

---

[2] Except if you grew up in Houston, which famously has no zoning.

variances (i.e. exceptions) that property owners can get.

7. Eminent Domain: The U.S. Constitution (as well as state constitutions) give the government the power to "take" private property away from the owner so long as the government is doing so for a public use and so long as it pays "just compensation." What is a public use though? And how do we figure out just compensation? Your Property class will answer these questions.

Before jumping into the details of these seven property doctrines, we should pause and answer a question that has vexed law students forever. . . .

3. What Is Blackacre?

Your professor is going to use a lot of hypothetical scenarios to teach you property law. That means she will need a hypothetical piece of land to use as an example. For hundreds of years, Property professors have called that imaginary piece of property "Blackacre." And when the hypothetical involves an adjoining piece of property, professors often call that land "Whiteacre" or "Greenacre" or some other color with the word "acre" tacked on at the end. None of these are real places.[3]

No one is sure where the term Blackacre comes from, but some speculate that it is named after the famous English legal commentator William Blackstone. Another theory is that Blackacre, Whiteacre, and the other colors matched crops grown on land (e.g. beans and potatoes). A simpler theory is that the names reflect what

---

[3] There was once a bar in Indiana started by some law students that was called Black Acre Brewing Company, but sadly it's now closed.

professors could draw on a chalkboard—the area inside the white lines was Whiteacre and the area outside the lines was Blackacre.

Whatever the origin, the most important thing for you to know is that you're not missing something important. If you were to change Blackacre to "Martian Mansion" or "Harry's House" all of the property rules you are learning would still be exactly the same. Basically, all you need to know is that Blackacre is just the name of a fictional piece of property.

4. Owning Property Now and in the Future: Present and Future Interests

One of the main property rights in the "bundle of sticks" is the ability to control what happens to your property. Think of it this way. You may want to sell your property, or give it away while you're alive, or direct what happens to it when you die. Many property owners have total control over what happens to their property. But not everyone. It depends on the type of estate you have.

If you acquired the property in "fee simple," you are a total boss and can do whatever you want. If you acquired the property as a "life estate," you have far less power. And if you have what's called "a defeasible fee," well that's just straight-up confusing. The law of what is called "estates and future interests" is intricate,[4] and I am just going to scratch the surface for you. Here are the broad strokes.

The Fee Simple Absolute: When someone buys or inherits property they usually get total control over it. In other words, most owners can sell their property, give it away, or devise it in their will to whoever they want. The law calls this fee simple absolute, or

[4] Confession: This section is right smack in the middle of the book. But it is the absolute last part of this book that I wrote. Why? Because future interests is hard.

often just "fee simple." If you've got property in fee simple, you're the boss. Live your best life and do whatever you want with your property.

The Fee Tail: Think back to feudal times of kings, queens, knights, and lords. (Or if you don't like history, just think of the HBO series *Game of Thrones*.) In those worlds, property owners didn't sell their property for cash so that they could retire to Florida. Instead, land was passed down from generation to generation. The fee tail provided an easy way to do this. When you acquired property in fee tail, you were the total and complete owner of the property. You could do whatever you wanted with it, except one thing. You couldn't sell or give it to the person of your choosing. Instead, a fee tail automatically transferred to your heirs upon your death.

You've probably noticed that the previous paragraph was written in the past tense. That's because the fee tail has been abolished in most of the United States. Yet, even though the fee tail is long gone, your professor will probably still discuss it. The reason is to help you understand that property law is not just about who occupies land, but about an owner's ability to direct what happens to their land.

Life Estate: The life estate gives the property owner the land for their life (or the length of someone else's life) but nothing further. After the "life" ends, the property goes elsewhere. So the person who possesses a life estate can *never* sell the property or give it away. The easiest way to think of this is to imagine a family—Lily and David get married, have a child named Cathy, and they all live a happy life. Decades go by and eventually David dies. A few years later, Lily meets someone new (let's call him Norm) and they get engaged. Norm moves into the home where Lily lived with David and raised Cathy. All is well, with only one problem, Norm's kids are jerks. Lily is concerned that if she dies before Norm that he will inherit her property and that eventually Norm's awful children will inherit her home, leaving her own child, Cathy, with nothing. At the same time, Lily doesn't want Norm to get kicked out of the house if she dies before him. Lily wants Norm to be able to keep living in the house; she just doesn't want it to end up in the hands of his awful kids. So instead of leaving either Norm or Cathy a fee simple she leaves Norm a life estate. If Lily dies first, Norm's life estate will allow him to own Lily's house and to continue to live there for the rest of his life. But there are two main limits on Norm's property ownership. First, he can't commit "waste," which is a fancy term for not being allowed to destroy or neglect the property. Second, Norm can't leave the house to his awful children. Instead, when Norm dies, the life estate will terminate, and the house will go back to Lily's heirs.

Defeasible Fees: Have you ever heard the phrase "no strings attached?" Well, a defeasible fee is the exact opposite. A person who acquires land as a defeasible fee gets the property with a major string that could mess up everything for them. And there are three types of defeasible fees. To keep matters simple though, I am not going to get into the details, just the basic concept.[5] The idea for all of the defeasible fees is that the new owner of the property gets total control, except if something happens. If that thing happens, the owner loses the property.

Here's an example: I am terribly allergic to cats, and I don't like them. I have never allowed any cats on my property, and I want it to stay that way. So instead of leaving my property to my heirs in fee simple, I put a restriction on it. I say "To Emily, I am retiring to Italy. Blackacre goes to you, so long as you never bring a cat onto the property." If Emily brings a cat on the property after I move to Rome, Blackacre will "revert" back to me. In other words, Emily

[5] Remember, this is just a big-picture book. But if you're really curious, the three defeasible fees are (1) fee simple determinable; (2) fee simple subject to condition subsequent; and (3) fee simple subject to executory limitation. Now are you glad we didn't get into the details?

owns Blackacre *for now*, but it might come back to me if she messes up and let's a cat onto the property.

But what if I'm really committed to retiring in Italy and never want to get Blackacre back? Another option would be for me to say "I give Blackacre to Emily, but if you ever bring a cat on the property, then Blackacre goes to your brother Ben."

The two examples above seem similar, but notice that there's a difference in where the property ends up. Your property professor will teach you the technical names for these scenarios. (Spoiler: the first is a possibility of reverter, while the second is an executory interest). The problem is that there are lots of other variations on defeasible fees, and as students get into the fine details, they often get lost. Your mission is to try not to lose track of the big picture. Defeasible fees are situations in which the new owner may lose control of the property if something forbidden happens.

5. Concurrent Estates

Sometimes, people co-own a piece of property. For example, a married couple can buy a house together. Or siblings might inherit property to be shared. Perhaps a few families go in together on buying a beach house. Often, co-owners split the property equally, but it doesn't have to be that way. The parties could arrange it so that one co-owner can owns 95% of the property while the other co-owner has only a 5% share.

Just because one owner only bought 5% of the property doesn't mean they only get to use 5% of the house though. Each co-owner has the right to possess and enjoy the whole property. So, the 95% owner can't tell the 5% owner that they are not allowed in the kitchen or the garage.

A sad reality of life is that the co-owners of property are not going to die at the same time. Your Property class is going to focus on what happens to co-owned property after someone dies. As you'll see, the answer depends on the type of ownership situation they have set up. There are three main co-ownership situations: Joint Tenancy, Tenancy by the Entirety, and Tenancy in Common.

Joint Tenancy: When a joint tenant dies, his share of the property automatically passes to the other joint tenant(s). The living joint tenant has a "right of survivorship." The great part of this arrangement is that the living joint tenant doesn't have to suffer through any unpleasant paperwork. No wills. No going to court. The surviving owner automatically becomes the sole owner of the property.

Tenancy by the Entirety is for married couples. As you'll learn in multiple law school courses, the law loves married couples and often provides them with extra benefits and protections. In a tenancy by the entirety, each married partner has a right of survivorship to the property. And if the couple gets in a fight, there is no option for one of them to sell their share to someone else. If Kourtney and Travis are married and have a tenancy by the entirety, and one decides to sell their interest in the property, that sale is null and void. Nor can one spouse "devise" or "leave" the property to someone else in the event of their death. In a tenancy by the entirety, the property has to pass to the spouse.

Tenancy in Common gives co-owners the most freedom to do what they want with their property. Each tenant in common owns an individual share of the property. The easiest example is when a few people co-own a beach house. Each tenant in common has the option to sell their share to someone else. Or a tenant in common could divide their share into multiple pieces. The other tenants in common can't stop them. Tenancy in common provides a co-owner with greater flexibility about what to do with their property, but notice that the property doesn't pass automatically when someone dies. The inheriting party must suffer through a lot of paperwork and perhaps some court appearances.

6. Landlord Tenant Law

If you've ever rented an apartment or house, you've almost certainly signed a lease that sets forth the terms of the rental agreement. That lease is a contract. Contracts control the rights that tenants have in most rental situations. But not all. Legislatures have used property law to provide some modest additional protection for tenants. The basic idea is that individual tenants have very little power compared to landlords, and thus the tenants need some extra help. As such, property law provides more robust protection for residential tenants (as opposed to commercial tenants like a hardware store) that goes beyond what is provided by their rental contract.

The main protections that property law provides for tenants are (1) the duty to deliver possession of the premises; (2) an implied covenant of quiet enjoyment; (3) an implied warranty of habitability; and (4) a prohibition on retaliatory eviction. Let's review them in a little more detail.

Imagine that Larry Landlord rents an apartment to Tonya Tenant. Landlord is obligated to make the premises available to Tonya. If Tonya's lease starts on January 1st and she arrives to find Larry's last tenant still in the apartment, Larry can't claim "Well, I delivered *legal* possession to you and now it's your job to evict the last tenant." Believe it or not, in the past, the landlord only had to deliver legal possession, not *actual* possession of the apartment. Today, that rule is long gone in America. If the old tenants have not vacated the apartment by January 1st, Larry Landlord has breached the duty to deliver possession.

Let's say that the apartment was available and that Tonya did in fact move in. However, later that day it started to rain and Tonya discovered that the roof leaked. A lot. Water was all over the apartment. Although Tonya's lease may not say anything about a dry apartment, property law has created an implied covenant of quiet enjoyment of the property. And "quiet" enjoyment is not just about there being no rock band practicing next door. If there are chronic problems that substantially interfere with Tonya getting to use the apartment, that is a breach of the covenant of quiet enjoyment.

What if things are even worse? Imagine that Tonya moves in and discovers that there is no running water or that there is no heat in the winter. The landlord has breached the implied warranty of habitability. The implied warranty of habitability imposes a duty on the landlord to keep the apartment in habitable condition.

Finally, what if Tonya tells the landlord about the problems and he does nothing. Tonya then reports the landlord to the Housing Authority. The landlord is now mad and says "Look, if you wanted a fancy apartment with a good roof, plumbing, and heat, you should have rented a more expensive place. You are evicted. Get out." Or perhaps the landlord decides to raise Tonya's rent because "she's such a troublemaker." All of Larry's responses are impermissible. The landlord cannot retaliate against Tonya for being a whistleblower and for insisting that the landlord comply with the rights she is afforded by law.

There are lots of other landlord-tenant topics that your professor might also cover. For instance, a federal statute called the Fair Housing Act prevents discrimination in how landlords decide who to rent to. You might also discuss the remedies for violations of the property rights discussed above and how "self-help" is ordinarily forbidden. Your professor might also focus on subleases or the ability to assign a lease to someone else. Property is such an enormous subject though that your professor may not have time for these subjects, so I'll just flag them here so that we can keep moving along.

7. Servitudes

A servitude is a non-possessory interest in land. Put another way, a servitude gives someone who is not the landowner the ability to do something with another person's land, or to prevent the owner from doing something their land. If you're like me and grew up in a traditional suburb, the concept of servitudes is going to sound strange. After all, if you own land with a home on it, it's your house and land, right? You get to do whatever you want with it, right? Not so fast.

There are different types of servitudes. I'm only going to introduce you to the three biggest ones you'll cover in Property—easements, restrictive covenants, and equitable servitudes—and help you understand where they come from, what they do, and how long they last.

a. Easements

Let's start with easements by thinking about a house on the ocean that backs up to the most beautiful beach you've ever seen. Everyone in town wants to get onto that beach, but this house is the only one that has a direct path. One resident in town says to the homeowner, "Look, I want to get on the beach. I'll pay you a lot of money if you will give me the right to walk across your land to get onto the beach." The homeowner agrees, the two parties write it down, and now we have what is called an affirmative easement. Your professor will go a step further and explain that the easement is in *gross*, rather than *appurtenant*. That means that the easement has been made in favor of a person rather than a neighboring pieces of land.

What's an easement appurtenant, and why do we care what is in gross and what's appurtenant? Imagine the same beach house, but this time imagine that there is a neighboring house. The neighbor doesn't need an easement to get to the beach, but the neighbor does need to run a cable across the other property in order to get internet service. The parties reach a deal exchanging cash for the cable line and an easement is created. This time the easement is *appurtenant* because it benefits a parcel of land. The cable is being used for the enjoyment of the neighbor's property.

Why do we care about the difference between easements in gross and easements appurtenant? Because easements appurtenant typically "run with the land." That means if either of the homeowners sell their property to someone else, the easement for the internet cable will remain in force. By contrast, someone who possesses an easement in gross usually can't transfer it to someone else.

So far, easements seem relatively simple—if people want to cross someone else's land they just pay for it. But things get more complicated quickly.

- Easements can also be by "necessity." If your next-door neighbor is land-locked, she will often have an easement by necessity to drive over your property and out to the road. And because it is by "necessity," the neighbor doesn't have to pay you for the easement.

- Prescriptive easements: If someone starts walking across your land without permission and keeps doing it for long enough, they can develop the right to keep walking over it forever. In other words, if you fail to notice and object, a person can develop a right to use your property without paying for it.

- Negative easements: All of our examples above are "affirmative" easements in which a party gets to do something on someone else's land. But you'll also learn about negative easements, which exist for four scenarios: light, air, support, or stream-water. Imagine an apartment building in New York City with a view of the Statute of Liberty. Now imagine a real estate developer wants to build a huge skyscraper across the street that would block the sunlight. If the apartment building has a negative easement, it can prevent the developer from building the skyscraper.[6]

b. Restrictive Covenants

Restrictive[7] covenants are a promise not to do something with the land. The idea sounds similar to a negative easement. But remember that negative easements are for very limited situations (light, air, support, or stream-water). Restrictive covenants can apply in more situations. For instance, your neighborhood might have restrictive covenants limiting the paint colors you can use, the type of mailbox you can put up, or forbidding a tin roof. Or maybe you have a restrictive covenant as a result of a contract with just one of your neighbors—say, a restrictive covenant that you won't keep more than three cars in your driveway.

Restrictive covenants are created by a contract, so it is not usually hard to figure out what the restriction actually is. Instead, the hard issue is whether the restrictive covenant "runs with the estate," which is just a way of asking whether the covenant continues when the property is sold or transferred to someone else.

---

[6] There are lots of other easement issues and details that you'll cover in a lot more detail in your Property class.

[7] There are other types of covenants, such as affirmative covenants. We're just sticking to the basics here though.

To figure out whether a covenant continues after the property is transferred or sold, you are going to analyze a bunch of factors, such as the intent of the parties and whether the covenant "touches and concerns the land" which is a fancy way of saying that the promise is about the land itself. Additionally, and most confusing, you will have to analyze something called "privity" which asks about the relationship between the original owners and the current owners. The question of when something runs with the land is too complicated to fully explain here, but I flag it so that you'll understand that this is the main issue you'll struggle with in learning about restrictive covenants.

c. Equitable Servitudes

A long time ago, there were separate courts for "law" and "equity" in the United States. If someone wronged you and you wanted to sue them for money damages, your claim was in "law." And if someone did something wrong and you wanted to prevent them from doing it again in the future, you would go to a court of equity and ask for an injunction. In other words, there were two sets of courts. Injunctions were awarded in courts of equity, whereas money damages were awarded in courts of law. Today, these different courts have been merged in most places across the country. So a plaintiff doesn't have to choose between going to a court for money damages and a different court for an injunction. While the divide between law and equity has disappeared in most respects, some terminology differences still persist, and "equitable" servitudes is one of those differences.

So, while the analysis of covenants and equitable servitudes is similar, the terminology still depends on what the plaintiff is asking for. Equitable servitudes are for injunctive relief.

8. Land Transactions

When land is sold, there is lots of paperwork to fill out. There are mortgage documents, tax forms, and insurance papers, to name just a few. Your Property professor probably won't go over all (or maybe even any) of this paperwork. But odds are that your professor will teach you about the different types of deeds to property and how to "record" those deeds so that everyone knows you are the new owner of the property.

a. Types of Deeds

First things first, a "deed" is a document that says you are the owner of a piece of property. There are three different types of deeds: (1) general warranty deeds; (2) special warranty deeds; and (3) quitclaim deeds.

Your first reaction might be, why are there different types of deeds? You either buy Blackacre or you don't, right? Shouldn't everyone get the same type of deed? Not always. Imagine that the last owner of Blackacre recently died and there are two wills, each of which left Blackacre to a different person. Now there's a dispute about who the true owner of Blackacre really is. In fancy property lingo, there is a cloud on the title.

Or consider the servitudes we learned about in the last section. What if the person buying Blackacre wants to be sure no one has an easement or a covenant that would restrict use of the property. In the past, a neighboring property had an easement to drive over Blackacre because a stream had washed out the neighbor's road. But after a drought, the stream has dried up, and now it seems like the old road *might* be usable again. Does the easement still exist? No one really knows. Things are uncertain.

The law has designed different deeds to deal with different levels of uncertainty for ownership of a piece of property. A general warranty deed says that the seller warrants that they have the ability to convey good title and that there are no liens, mortgages or servitudes on the property. If you're buying property, a general warranty deed is the best deed you can get. A special warranty deed gives the purchaser the same warranties, but only for problems that cropped up during the time when the seller owned the property.

A quitclaim deed is the riskiest kind of deed. When the seller gives you the property with a quitclaim deed, she is making no representations at all. It's like the seller saying "Hey, I'll sell this to you, but I might not even own it, and you're taking all the risk here." Now, why would someone agree to a quitclaim deed? Personally, I wouldn't, because it's too risky. But the risk might be worth it for some people. Maybe the buyer is getting the property at a huge price discount and is willing to take the risk.

b. Recording

Now that you've paid money for a house and gotten a deed in exchange, your real estate deal is done. But the process is not completely finished. Now, it is time to "record" your deed. Just because I have a deed to Blackacre does not mean anyone else in the world will know it. So governments have set up recording systems in which you file your deed with the government so that anyone can look up who owns which piece of property. That way, everyone is on the same page.

Why might your Property professor focus on the recording system? It's not for the ordinary case. Normally, an owner sells the property to one person and everything is "on the up and up." But not always. Sometimes there is an evil "double dealer." Imagine that Oliver (the owner of Blackacre) sells it to Allison. And then a week later, Oliver sells Blackacre to Betty. Now who owns Blackacre? The answer is that "it depends."

About half the states in the United States have "notice" recording statutes. If Allison never recorded her deed to Blackacre, then Betty would have no notice that Allison had bought it. Betty would reasonably believe that Oliver still owned Blackacre. That would make Betty a bona fide purchaser who lacked notice of Allison's earlier purchase. Under a notice statute, Betty wins and will become the owner of Blackacre. This makes sense. After all, Allison could have recorded her deed. She's the least cost avoider.

The other half of states have a "race notice statute." Under that statute we ask if Betty is *both* a bona fide purchaser and whether she recorded her deed first. If so, she wins. But if Allison records her deed before Betty makes it to the courthouse, Allison wins.

Once again, your Property professor will probably focus not just on the rules, but also on the goals of property law. The recording statutes ensure certainty and productive use of the land.

9. Zoning

One of the main jobs of government is to protect the health, safety, and general welfare of the public. It also doesn't hurt for your city to look nice! Government has zoning rules to accomplish all of these tasks on behalf of the community. To appreciate what zoning does, think of what your hometown would look like if there were no zoning rules. One homeowner might decide to build a ten-story house that towers over all the two-story homes of her neighbors. A corporation might buy a few lots in the middle of your block and build a smelly chemical plant. A strip club might open next to an elementary school. Or a loud bar might play live music until 3:00am right next to a retirement community. Can you imagine the fighting that would ensue between angry residents, chemical plant executives, strip clubs, and rock bands?

Zoning rules bring order and thus improve the general welfare for the community. The first step is for the zoning rules to set up a board—often called a Zoning Board—that will designate different areas for different types of use. For instance, a city might designate zones for green space (e.g. parks), residential, commercial, and industrial uses. Or it could adopt even more detailed rules that separate residential zoning into single-family homes, multi-family homes, and mixed residential and commercial use where apartments are mixed in next to a high-end grocery store. There are lots of possibilities. The point is not for you to memorize each of the zones in your hometown, but to understand that the zoning board has created a comprehensive plan in advance to set up how land will generally be used.

Property owners can then ask for exceptions to the zoning rules, which are known as "variances." The two main types of variances are "area variances" and "use variances." An area variance is typically for modest exceptions to zoning rules. For example, imagine that a zoning rule says that fences are not allowed to be visible from the street. (That rule is designed to make the neighborhood look beautiful and consistent.) But our property owner has a particular need for a fence. Perhaps she is blind and needs to have a seeing-eye dog that can be let outside in a fenced-in area. Our property owner may be entitled to an area variance if she can demonstrate an undue hardship and that the variance won't diminish the property values of her neighbors. Basically, she has to really need the fence and it can't be so ugly or out of place as to harm the neighbors. Area variances are often granted.

By contrast, use variances are rarely granted. Imagine that a property owner lives in an area zoned for single-family homes. After school, he babysits ten neighborhood children whose parents work all day. The property owner has decided he'd like to charge some money for all the babysitting, but of course his house is zoned for residential use, not commercial use. He can't just open a daycare. Our homeowner would ask for a use variance. To be successful, he will have to show special circumstances. His odds of prevailing are not good.

10. Eminent Domain or "Takings"

Remember that one of the key purposes of property law is to maximize the productive use of land. One way to do that is for the government to build roads, bridges, schools, and other structures that enable cities to thrive. A public school might benefit thousands of children. A highway could benefit millions of people in a busy city. Those projects are hard to build though if a single piece of private property is in the way of the school or highway.

To deal with this problem, the U.S. Constitution and state constitutions specifically give the federal, state, and local governments the power to take private property. This is called "eminent domain" or "takings," and there is good reason for this government power. If we let just one private property owner refuse to sell, they could block the highway or school from being built and stand in the way of progress. Or, if the government didn't have the power of eminent domain, the holdout might eventually sell their land, but only after demanding a ridiculously high price that drives up the price of the school or highway.

Eminent domain prevents a landowner from completely blocking the highway or running up the price. In a way, the private property owner is the "least cost avoider." Sure, it sucks for the private property owner to lose their preferred location, but it is better for everyone else if the highway is built.

America was founded on the ideals of liberty and freedom from government overreach. So there are some students—you may be one—who think that eminent domain is unjust or even outrageous.

You've got to put that aside though. Your Property exam isn't going to ask about your personal opinion of eminent domain. What matters is that you understand how it works and what the main limitations of it are.

The first main limitation is that the government can't just take the private property and walk away. The Constitution requires the government to pay "just compensation" for any private property that it takes. Courts determine "just compensation" by figuring out the fair market value of the property. If the government wasn't taking the property, what would a reasonable buyer pay for it?

The second limitation is that the taking must be for a public use. This turns out not to be much of a limitation. Obviously, a highway is public use. But what if private land could be better used if the government gave it to a different private owner to use as part of a comprehensive development plan? Can that be a public use? It might surprise you to learn that the answer is "Yes." In an infamous Supreme Court case called *City of New London v. Kelo* (2005), the city used eminent domain to take property from homeowners and transfer it to a private entity that planned to revitalize an economically distressed area. The private entity was going to build a research facility for a pharmaceutical company and a riverwalk with stores, restaurants, and housing. The homeowners argued that turning distressed private property into nicer private property was not a "public use." The Supreme Court disagreed however, saying that economic development is a public use. The Court thus adopted a very broad "public use" doctrine.

So far, we have talked about the classic type of eminent domain where the government physically removes a landowner from their property. You should also be aware that there is also a doctrine called "regulatory takings." Sometimes, the government passes a law or regulation that limits the way that a property owner can use their property, even if it doesn't entirely throw them off their land. Can that be a "taking?" The answer is "sometimes."

Here's an example: Imagine that you buy an empty beachfront lot intending to build a house on it when you retire. Sadly, the year after you buy the lot, terrible beach erosion develops along the coastline. To reduce the problem, the city passes a regulation that says no one can build a new home on the beachfront. Your beachfront lot is now pretty much useless. Sure, you can sit in a lawn chair and look at the ocean. But that's not worth much. People buy beachfront land to build a beach house! The government may have to pay you just compensation.

By contrast, imagine that the government passes a different regulation to protect the shoreline. The regulation states that no one is allowed to build within 20 feet of the shoreline. You have a large lot and you can still build a house. It's just that the house will have to be smaller than you wanted in order for it to comply with the 20-foot restriction. You can still get a reasonable return on your investment and thus there has been no regulatory taking and you are not entitled to any compensation.

Points to Remember

- As you learn different property doctrines, consider the theoretical reasons courts think about in creating property rules. Consider the reasonable expectations of the parties, who would be the least cost avoider, and what rules would result in productive use of the land. Sometimes those theories will conflict.
- Think of property rights as a bundle of sticks. Not all property owners have the same rights. For example, whether you can sell your property depends on what kind of property interests you have.
- Blackacre is not a real place.

- You can own property in fee simple (with total control over it), as a life estate (where the ownership is limited to someone's lifetime), or as a defeasible fee (where you can lose the property if a specified event happens).
- There are three ways for people to concurrently own the same piece of property: (1) joint ownership with a right of survivorship that automatically passes upon death; (2) tenancy by the entirety for married couples; and (3) tenancy in common, in which nothing happens automatically and the owners can decide what happens to their shares.
- Most tenants sign a lease and thus landlord-tenant disputes are usually governed by contract law. However, your Property course will show you some additional protections for residential tenants to prevent them from being mistreated. They are (1) the landlord's duty to deliver possession of the premises; (2) an implied covenant of quiet enjoyment; (3) an implied warranty of habitability; and (4) a prohibition against retaliatory eviction.
- Servitudes include easements, restrictive covenants, and equitable servitudes. All of these are non-possessory interests. The person who holds the servitude can't kick anyone off their land, but they can use the land or prevent the owner from doing something with the land.
- When you buy property you get a deed that conveys title. General warranty deeds promise that the owner has the right to sell the property and that there are no liens, mortgages, or servitudes. Special warranty deeds promise that no problems cropped up during the seller's ownership period. And quitclaim deeds promise nothing. Once a buyer gets the deed, they must record it in order to give notice to the rest of the world that they are the new property owner.

- Most cities and towns are organized into zones so that there are different areas for residential, commercial, and industrial property. The goal is to make the city look good and have it run safely and efficiently. If a property owner wants to do something forbidden by the zoning ordinance, they can request a variance.
- Government can use eminent domain to take private property for public use if it pays just compensation to the owners. Eminent domain includes the power to take property from one private landowner and to give it to another private party.
- When a government regulation renders property useless, it amounts to a taking and the government must pay just compensation.

CHAPTER 8

Legal Research and Writing

Lawyers have to know a lot of law. There's a reason why you spend an entire year learning all of the 1L subjects we covered in the last six chapters. But just knowing the law is not valuable if you cannot communicate what you know. To be a good lawyer, you must also be a good communicator. Communication comes in a lot of forms—storytelling, oral arguments in court, lengthy written memos, emails, even text messages. Your Legal Research and Writing course—"LRW" for short—is going to teach you how to be an effective communicator.

Now, you might be tempted to say "This will be easy. I'm already a great writer." That's possible, but unlikely. I hate to burst your bubble, but most high schools and colleges don't force students to do enough writing to make them great. Moreover, the papers you have written in History, Literature, and other courses are not the same as the kind of legal writing you will do in law school and as a lawyer. You haven't had to figure out how to present facts succinctly, or how to take precedent from other cases and apply it. Nor have you figured out how to organize inter-connected legal concepts in the clearest order.

Plus, your LRW course is not limited to writing. You will also learn how to conduct legal research. There is no large book that has the answer to every legal question. Instead, you will need to figure out how to unearth the right cases and statutes. And that requires understanding how to dig up legal principles from law review articles, treatises, regulations, online databases, and a host of other sources. Additionally, once you find the right cases, statutes, and regulations you need to know how to cite them correctly, which is another topic in your LRW course.[1] As Yoda said in one of the Star Wars movies, "Much to learn you still have."[2]

1. Why Legal Writing Is Unique

Let's step back and look at the big picture of what you'll be learning in your LRW course. While you'll have to use proper sentence structure, spelling, and punctuation, legal writing is about much more. Your professor will focus heavily on analysis, research, and organizing your thoughts in a clear and compelling way.

The other major difference between legal writing and "regular" writing is the audience. Think of great pieces of writing, like the Gettysburg Address or the President Kennedy's speech in which he urged people to "ask not what your country can do for you, but what you can do for your country." Those speeches were written for a mass audience. Lawyers write for busy judges, opposing counsel, and clients. When the audience has different needs, your writing must adapt. Your LRW course will teach you to focus on the purpose of your writing. As I'll explain in more detail below, your purpose may be to predict and clarify the legal answer, or it may be to persuade.

---

1 Legal citations follow something called "The Bluebook."

2 It wasn't one of the good Star Wars movies, but the point still holds. *See* Star Wars, Episode II—Attack of the Clones (Lucasfilm 2002). Also, just to be extra dorky, I'll note that the citation is in proper Bluebook format!

Because there is a unique and well-developed audience for legal writing, lawyers have developed a shared *method* of writing. Legal writing organizes complex thoughts around rules and principles. The name of the method may vary slightly based on your instructor, but it will be some version of CREAC, which stands for "Conclusion, Rule, Explanation, Application, Conclusion."[3]

The core idea is that you tell the reader the conclusion up front. Then you follow the conclusion with the guiding principle—the rule. After that, you explain to your reader how that rule has been applied in the past in prior cases (the explanation). Then, you show the reader how the facts of your case compare to the facts and rationale of those prior cases (the application). Finally, you reiterate your conclusion.

Whether your case is about a basic criminal law issue or a complicated rule governing the regulation of nuclear waste, the format is the same. Think of the CREAC approach like a Haiku. A haiku poem can be about any topic at all, but the format is always the same. There are 17 syllables—five in the first line, seven in the second line, and five in the third line. The format is always the same. The CREAC approach to legal writing always uses the same format as well.

Once you understand the CREAC formula, you'll learn to apply it to the two big categories of legal writing: (1) objective writing (sometimes also called "predictive writing") and (2) persuasive writing. These categories are so different and so important that many law schools often dedicate an entire semester to each one. Let's walk through them.

---

[3] Other variations include IRAC (Issue, Rule, Application, Conclusion) and CRAC (Conclusion, Rule, Application, Conclusion).

2. Predictive/Objective Writing

Predictive/objective is writing designed to show the likely outcome of a case or a specific issue. The audience for predictive/objective writing is usually internal. Think of the busy supervising partner in a law firm who needs to know how a judge is likely to decide a particular legal question. The supervising partner asks the junior lawyer to write a memo "predicting" the outcome of an issue. The memo is to educate the supervising partner about the law and how the facts of the case would apply to that legal issue. The supervising partner doesn't need to be persuaded. Instead, she needs to be informed. The supervising partner needs to understand how an issue is likely to come out so that she knows whether it would be better to settle or go to trial. Even the best lawyers in the world can't possibly know every legal nuance off the top of their head. To inform their clients, the best lawyers still need objective legal analysis that helps them predict how a case will unfold.

Because a predictive/objective memo is designed to inform an internal audience, your professor is going to drum into you that there should be no spin in it. The idea is that the memo should present the issue straight down the middle, as even-handed as possible. This is what is meant by the memo being "objective."

No matter where you go to law school, your professor is likely to cover the same core components of a predictive/objective memo:

- The Caption says who wrote the memo, who it is addressed to, the subject matter, and the date. This is easy stuff, so it looks bad if you get it wrong. Be careful here.
- The Question Presented/Issue Presented lets the reader know what legal issue is being addressed and what key critical facts apply.

- Brief Answer/Short Answer presents an abbreviated answer to the Question Presented/Issue Presented, including the applicable rule, jurisdiction, and an outline of the analysis.
- The Statement of Facts is a section that neutrally relays the key facts of the case. Remember, no spinning. Present it neutrally.
- Discussion: This is where you apply the facts to the law. You will use the CREAC structure we described above to help you walk through your analysis methodically and fully. This is the longest section of a memo.
- The Conclusion should be a short summary of how you think the court will resolve the major issue you are dealing with.

Your major assignment for predictive/objective writing will be the memo described above. There are shorter types of objective writing as well though. Your professor may show you how to write an email memo or even how to text an objective/predictive analysis.

3. Persuasive Writing

Now that we have a handle on an objective memo, let's move on and consider persuasive writing. As I said above, many law schools have a full-year legal writing course in which the professor covers the objective memo in the first semester and focuses on persuasive writing in the second semester.

Unlike predictive/objective writing (which is for an internal audience), the audience for persuasive writing is external. You may be writing for the judge who will be deciding a disputed legal question. Or you may be writing for opposing counsel who will be recommending to their client whether to settle a case rather than pushing forward to trial. Persuasive writing is not "straight down the middle" writing. Instead, you are trying to persuade the reader of a particular answer. Spinning is perfectly fine and indeed it's probably a good idea. Obviously, you cannot lie about what a case, regulation, or statute says. But when there is room for interpretation you can shape the law to your side's advantage As long as you stay within the bounds of the legal ethics rules,[4] you can spin cases, in an effort to convince the judge that your interpretation of the law is correct.

The persuasive brief contains slightly different components than the objective memo:

- The Caption sits at the top of the first page of your briefs and other court filings. It includes the names of the parties, the name of the court that is hearing the case, and the docket number (which the court creates to keep track of all the documents in the case). Like the caption in an objective memo, this information is all simple. Proofread carefully to make sure you don't make an embarrassing mistake.

- The Issue Statement or Introduction briefly presents the legal questions in the way that best suits your side.

- The Statement of Facts is crucial and much more difficult to do well than you might think. Stories can be weaved in lots of different ways and from different perspectives. You want to set out the facts in a way that is honest, but which portrays your client's side in the most positive light. In particular,

[4] All lawyers are bound by the rules of professional responsibility. During your 2L or 3L year you will probably take a class specifically focusing on the legal ethics rules.

once you know the legal rules at issue, you want to shape the facts in a way that will fit with the interpretation of the legal rules that you are proposing.

- The Argument section is where you set out the relevant law and apply it to the facts of the case. Because this is a persuasive document for the judge as your audience you should present the legal precedents in the most favorable light you can. You may use the CREAC structure, but you may also deviate from the that structure to argue effectively.
- The Conclusion should be short and sweet. Your professor will probably suggest that you state something like "For the foregoing reasons, this court should grant summary judgment" or something like that.

The classic type of persuasive writing is a brief that you submit to a court. But it is not the only type. You will learn how to write demand letters, settlement letters, and other documents in which you advocate on behalf of a client outside of the court setting.

4. How to Succeed in Your Legal Writing Class

By now, it should be pretty clear that your legal writing class is a different animal than your other 1L courses. The good news is that, in all likelihood, there will be no final exam for you to take. And that means there is no outline for you to write. Nice! However, that puts some pressure on you to do well on your memo, brief, and other writing projects. How do you do that?

a. *Slow and Steady Work Is Really Important*

Many of us—myself included—wrote some of their college papers at the last minute. When I was a college student at the University of Delaware, there was a fantastic pizza place in back of my dorm and it was open late. Did I start some of my papers the night before while I had midnight pizza? The answer is "Yes. Yes, I did." Did that turn out okay? "Yes. Yes, it did." Can you take that approach in law school? "Not if you want to get a good grade."

Writing a legal memo or brief requires research. It involves a totally new writing style. It requires that you get the citation format correct. And it is graded by professors who are specifically focused on writing and who are lawyers. I'm not saying your history or political science professor wasn't smart or a good writer. But the reality is that your legal writing professor will be laser focused on your writing. You cannot write a brief at midnight and get it passed your legal writing professor.

b. *Make Checklists*

As we'll discuss in Chapter 13, you will be writing outlines of legal rules for your other 1L courses. You don't have to do that for your legal writing course. But you should write a checklist of the things you've noticed during the semester. And in particular, you should be on the lookout for your own weaknesses and put them in the checklist. Let me explain in more detail.

If you are doing your memo or your brief correctly, you will write lots of drafts. The goal is to refine and improve each draft so that it is better than the last. You could do that by just generally reading each new draft and generally editing it. But that's not the ideal way to proceed. Instead, you should devote your revisions and new drafts to topics your professor focused on during the semester. For example, odds are that your professor will tell you horror stories of lawyers who spelled the judge's name incorrectly. Your professor may also instruct you to use a party's full name the first time you reference them in a memo or brief and then to use just their last name for every subsequent mention. Your professor will also probably spend a lot of time teaching you how to write strong topic sentences and how to avoid the passive voice. You should create a checklist that lists these concepts:

- Spelling of parties, cases, and the judge.
- Full name first, then last name in subsequent references
- Strong topic sentences
- Avoid passive voice

These are not the only concepts your professor will cover, but you get the idea. As you edit your brief, you should do a separate pass through for each of the bullet points above. Instead of just generally re-reading your memo or brief, you should read with one of the specific bullet-point purposes listed above. Then you should read the draft again with the next specific bullet-point purpose in mind. And so on.

When you get back assignments or work with your professor on rough drafts, write down the areas you have trouble with. Do not just say to yourself "I will do better next time." Don't assume that you'll remember what your weak spots were. Instead, add your personal weaknesses to your checklist. The goal here is to systemize your writing.

Additionally, you should also create a checklist for each of the sections of your memo. For instance, list all the main concepts that your professor taught you about how to shape your Statement of Facts. Your professor likely will have given you advice about what to do and not do as you write your Statement of Facts section. Create a checklist of that advice so that you can draft and review your memo with that in mind. And do the same for the Rule, Application, and other sections of your memo.

Now, you might be saying to yourself, "Does my professor really expect me to do a separate review and edit of my draft for spelling, topic sentences, Statement of Facts, Analysis, and all the other concepts listed above? That would amount to me reading the draft more than a dozen times." The answer is "Yes, they do." And if you further reaction is "Wouldn't that take a lot of time?" The answer is "Yes, it does." And that's why you can't write your memo or brief the night before.

c. *Avoid Passive Voice*

You'll notice that one of the checklist items above was "passive voice." This topic is really important, so let me say a little more about it. If I write that "A car accident happened" that is passive voice. Similarly, if my brief says that "mistakes were made" that is also passive voice. Notice that the subject is missing and that the verb is not actively telling you what happened.

Passive voice conveys some information, but not as much as if you write in an active format. Additionally, when you use passive voice your writing is just not as sharp. Just ask Billy Joel, whose first draft was "The Fire Was Not Started"[5] before he got rid of the passive voice and called it "We Didn't Start the Fire."

Passive voice crops up frequently in legal writing because you are dealing with complicated legal concepts and complicated facts. When you're not 100% sure what the legal standard is or what exactly happened in the case, you may be tempted to cut corners. Sometimes, you may even do this subconsciously. The easiest way to cut corners is to remove the subject and active voice.

---

[5] This is a joke. Billy Joel is cool and would never use the passive voice.

Your legal writing professor will teach you to use active voice because it conveys more information and does so more clearly. You need to be clear who the subject of the sentence is and who did what. So you must avoid passive voice. The best way to avoid passive voice is to read through your memo or brief with your radar up specifically to find passive voice.

d. *Avoid Legalese*

When people think of legal writing they often use the derogatory term "legalese." When a non-lawyer wants to act like a lawyer (or make fun of one) they sometimes say things like: "In as much as I have heretofore enunciated the governing principles, I will hereinafter state them deliberately." Legalese is using a lot of big words to say very little. Unfortunately, you will encounter some of this dense and painful writing in your 1L courses. Some of the cases you read in Torts, Contracts, Property, and Criminal Law will be very old and will include wordy sentences filled with legalese.

You may be tempted to use legalese in your own writing. Don't do it. As the book *Plain English for Lawyers* explains, legalese is wordy, unclear, pompous, and dull. In the real world, lawyers do not talk or write with legalese. To the extent you see legalese in cases you read in your 1L classes, remember that those cases are from a time gone by. Today, there is a consensus in favor of plain English writing. Your legal writing professor doesn't want to see any legalese, nor will your future employer. Just use plain English.

e. *Proofread the Right Way*

The final step before you submit your assignment is to proofread what you have written. It is actually very hard to proofread your own work though. The reason is that our mind auto-corrects our own writing for us. Look at this very messy example:

> Aoccdrnig to a rscheearch at Cmabrigde Uinervtisy, it deosn't mttaer in waht oredr the ltteers in a wrod are, the olny iprmoetnt tihng is taht the frist and lsat ltteer be at the rghit pclae. The rset can be a toatl mses and you can sitll raed it wouthit porbelm. Tihs is bcuseae the huamn mnid deos not raed ervey lteter by istlef, but the wrod as a wlohe.

Of course, your writing is not going to be this sloppy. But the point in the block quote (which I trust you can in fact read) is definitely true. When you sit back in a chair and just run your eyes across a screen, you will miss all kinds of tiny mistakes.

The obvious way to deal with this problem in the real world is to have another person proofread your work (and for you to do the same for them). Because you are being graded in your legal writing course though, the odds are that your professor will not allow your classmate to proofread your draft. So you have to find another way to proofread. Here is an old-fashioned suggestion: Print out your draft and read it with a ruler. Go word by word instead of just running your eyes across a screen.

5. Dealing with Writer's Block

No chapter on legal writing would be complete without discussing writer's block. As you sit down to write your memo, brief, or any other assignment, you will start by staring at a blank page. Some people have no problem dealing with this. Others find it horrifying. In particular, law school sometimes attracts perfectionists who have trouble putting down mediocre words on a page to start with.

Here are some strategies to deal with writer's block:

- Break your project down into smaller pieces. Start with the smallest bite.

- Write down the parts that you do know. Often in law school, you will deal with complicated legal concepts. You may have a firm grasp of some of the material, but not all of it. If you are struggling because you don't understand all of the law you have to analyze, just start by writing what you do know. If you are struggling because you know the rule but not how to apply it to the facts, then just start by writing the rule. Get down on paper what you can.
- Find an accountability partner. When people are struggling with writing they sometimes avoid it. They might think "things will be better later and I'll wait until then." But this mode of thinking leads to students waiting until the last minute. So force yourself to start writing, even if you don't think you're ready yet. An accountability partner who sits with you while you write is a good trick to make you start writing. If you have a fellow 1L who you can do this with, great. If not, then you can use Zoom to be on a videocall with a non-law school friend.
- Use a throwaway document. If you have gotten into a bad mindset and are convinced that you won't be able to write anything good, then give yourself permission to write something bad. Tell yourself to just write something and that if turns out bad, you can delete it. Give yourself permission to write something bad. Often, some of the writing in your throwaway document will actually be quite good. You can then just cut and paste that good writing into a different document.
- Write about "what you will say." Sometimes, you will know in your head what you want to say, but you

can't find the right words when it is time to start typing. To nudge yourself along, begin your sentences with "I will say." For instance, "I will say that this is not burglary because it was daytime and burglary requires the actions to be at night." Later on, you can go back and delete the "I will say."

- Set a timer. If you are really stuck, you can set a timer for 10 minutes (or some other reasonably short time) and force yourself to write for that entire time. If you have nothing to say you can start by just writing "words, words, words." Remember, you can always delete irrelevant sentences. Once you start typing though, you will often begin to focus and be able to start writing relevant and coherent sentences.
- Don't edit your work while drafting. A famous quote (often attributed to Ernest Hemingway) is that you should "write drunk and edit sober." I'm not encouraging you to write your memo while drunk. Instead, I'm just encouraging you to get something down on paper. Perfectionists often get stuck because they don't want to move on until a sentence or paragraph is perfect. Resist that urge. You can clean up your writing later. Give yourself permission to write a bad draft.

6. Legal Research: The Big Picture

In addition to legal writing, you are also going to learn how to conduct legal research in your 1L class. You will learn from professors and librarians who are way better at research than me. So I am only going to give you the big picture.

There are three main legal research tools that law students and lawyers use to look for the answers to legal questions: Westlaw, Lexis-Nexis, and Bloomberg.[6] You can use these tools to search broadly, or you can use them to search particular databases that are much more specific. For instance, in Westlaw you can search through a database of "All Cases" that enables you to run your search through practically every judicial decision in the country. But that search is usually too big, so you can narrow it down to a smaller database. Perhaps you only want to search federal cases. Or maybe just federal cases in one particular section of the country (what you'll learn is called a "federal circuit"). Or perhaps you only care about federal cases from Indiana. The databases operate like a funnel, allowing you to search broadly or narrowly.

Additionally, there are databases besides judicial decisions. You can look through databases that focus on treatises, or news stories, or regulations, or statutes. If you thought Google, YouTube, and Reddit could show you all the information on Earth you were wrong. Westlaw, Lexis-Nexis, and Bloomberg contain a ton of additional information that is sitting beyond an expensive paywall. And your law school is going to give you access to all of it for free.

The challenge is understanding how to use the databases effectively. Most students have grown up googling the answer to questions. You are probably accustomed to writing some key words in a search box and then sifting through the results to find the best answer. The legal research databases provide you with a similar option. If you are looking for how courts have interpreted the element of "nighttime" in a burglary statute, you will be tempted to open the "All Cases" database and then type in key terms like "darkness," "moonlight," and "pitch black" in the hopes of finding a case that says something like "To constitute a burglary the prosecution need not prove that it was pitch black outside or that

---

6 I say "main" because there are other databases for specialized areas of law.

the moon had fully risen. Total darkness is not required." You could certainly search for law that way, but it would return a ton of irrelevant results that would take an eternity to go through. And those results might not even include the cases you are really looking for.

Instead, you should search by looking for the correct topical area of law and then narrowing down the funnel. You might start in the treatises database. That will include books by law professors and something called the American Law Reports ("ALR's"), which catalog cases by subject area. These sources will have already gathered the most important cases in a particular area. You can then plug in the leading cases from the treatises and ALR's and see what newer cases (hopefully ones in your jurisdiction) have cited those leading cases. In addition to treatises and ALR's, you might also look through the law review database to look for scholarly articles. Perhaps you will find an article that sets forth how the law of burglary has developed over time. A related approach is to pull up the relevant statute and to look at something called "Notes of Decisions" which takes apart the statute section-by-section and summarizes the leading cases by topic.

It's too early for you to understand in detail how to use all of these approaches. Indeed, you will probably forget most of the suggestions in the paragraph above. The key point you should remember though is that legal research is not the same thing as googling something with a search engine. You want to funnel your research downward by starting with the experts who have already sifted through a ton of judicial decisions.

7. Learning Citation Rules

Your Legal Research and Writing course will also probably teach you how to cite cases, statutes, and other legal rules correctly. The field of law uses something called The Bluebook as its citation guide. The Bluebook is a long and tedious text that shows you the proper citation style for what seems like a million different scenarios. Students often hate the Bluebook because they think it is unnecessary minutiae that is a waste of their time. I am not going to dispute that the Bluebook can be tedious and painful, but I think it's also important to understand that the Bluebook teaches you useful skills that actually go beyond proper formatting.

Here's the key point. The citation rules in the Bluebook are not arbitrary and illogical. The citations are there to convey important information about the cases, statutes, and regulations you are citing. To understand this, you have to go back to a time before online databases. Back in the day, legal research was done in hard-copy books. You couldn't surf from one case to the other, or click on a link in an online case to be able to read a statute that was being referred to in the case. Instead, you had to go and find the book where the case, statute, or regulation was written. And to find those, you needed to use the citation. The citations are like a treasure map.

For instance, imagine you are reading a case and you see a reference to another case that seems perfect for the argument you are working on. That case (which I've made up) is cited as follows:

United States v. Jones, 127 F.3d 485 (4th Cir. 1997)

That citation actually conveys a lot of useful information. First, it tells you that one of the parties is the United States, which probably means it is a criminal case. Next, it tells you that the case is located in the "F.3d" books. The letter "F" is an abbreviation for a series of books called the Federal Reporter. The series runs from volume 1 to 999. When it reaches the end it starts over in a new series. The "3d" thus tells us it is in the 3rd series of the Federal Reporter. The Federal Reporter includes only cases by the federal appellate courts. Additionally, the citation tells you what section of the country the case comes from. We know this because the "4th

Cir" refers to the U.S. Court of Appeals for the Fourth Circuit (the section of the country that includes Maryland, North Carolina, South Carolina, Virginia, and West Virginia). The "1997" obviously refers to the year the case was decided. And for location purposes the number 127 tells us that we'll find that case in volume 127, and the number 485 tells us that the case starts on page 485.

The citation tells us how to find the case, but it also tells us how valuable the case might be. If we are litigating a state law case in Wyoming, then federal decisions from the east coast probably aren't that important. If we are litigating that same state case in South Carolina, well a federal decision from the circuit that covers South Carolina will probably be persuasive, even if it's not binding. And if we're litigating a federal case in South Carolina, then a favorable decision from the Fourth Circuit is like hitting the jackpot. The only thing more useful would be a case from the U.S. Supreme Court. We know all of this without even reading a word of the actual judicial decision. The citation includes valuable clues, if you know how to understand them.

Points to Remember

- Most legal writing uses the same structure. In most law schools, this is taught as CREAC—Conclusion, Rule, Explanation, Application, Conclusion.
- You will start your legal writing course by focusing on predictive/objective writing. The audience for predictive/objective writing is internal—often a supervising lawyer from your law firm. Your goal is to give neutral analysis so that the other lawyer knows the strengths and weaknesses of the case. No spin!
- The second type of writing you will learn is persuasive writing. The audience for persuasive writing is external—often judges or opposing counsel. Persuasive writing is not "straight down

the middle." It is okay to spin cases and facts as long as you are not dishonest or deceptive.

- The memo or brief for your legal writing course is not like a college paper. Legal writing is harder and requires you to synthesize more concepts than a college paper. It also requires a lot of editing. You cannot leave it until the last minute.
- To edit, you should not just re-read your memo or brief over and over again. You should make checklists with the core concepts that your professor covered during the semester and review the draft one time for each of those concepts. Read once for spelling. Read another time for topic sentences. Read yet another time to look for passive voice.
- If you suffer from writer's block, implement strategies specifically designed to get words on the page. Break your project down into smaller bites and start with the easiest ones. If you don't know everything you need to cover, then write down the concepts you do know. Find an accountability partner who you can sit with—in person or virtually—to make you keep writing. Use a throwaway document to give yourself permission to get bad words on a page. If you can't find a good way to start a sentence, write down what "I will say." Set a timer for 10 minutes and force yourself to write until the timer goes off.

CHAPTER 9

Briefing Cases and Preparing for Class

It's time to prepare for class. I am going to suggest you take three steps to prepare for class: (1) read carefully; (2) brief the cases; and (3) think about whether the cases make sense. After describing these three steps in more detail, I'm going to give you a real (and interesting!) case that I cover in my Criminal Law class for you to read, brief, and think about.

1. Step 1: Read Carefully

Most of your reading assignments will consist of excerpts from judicial opinions. You obviously know that you will have to read the assigned cases. But there are different ways to read. In college, you might have skimmed the reading to look for the key paragraph. You can admit it. You used to skim in college. I know you did it because I did it too!

For reasons that are already probably clear, you can't skim in law school. Law school focuses not just on the conclusion but on the reasoning that led to the conclusion. So you need to understand the legal doctrines that the court relies on. Additionally, the facts are really important in law school cases. Sometimes one or two facts can turn the outcome of a case in a different direction. And the court does not hang out a sign that says, "critical facts right here." You have to read carefully to spot the critical facts. Here are some do's and don'ts for reading.

- *Do* read slowly.
- *Do* read passages a second time if you didn't understand them.
- *Do* read passages a second time if your mind wandered. Let's be honest: some cases are boring. You're going to lose focus occasionally. That's fine. But go back over the parts of the case where you zoned out.
- *Do* look up words if you see something you don't understand. Judicial decisions often contain Latin words and phrases as shorthand for legal doctrines. If you don't know a word or phrase, look it up.
- *Do* take notes in the margin of the casebook if that helps you think about the facts and reasoning.
- *Do* feel free to underline or star key passages.
- *Don't* skip block quotes that are indented. For some reason, when a long quote is indented into a block, people psychologically have the desire to skip over it. Don't do that.
- *Don't* paint the page yellow with a highlighter. Using a highlighter is fine, but don't highlight everything on the page and feel like you understand the case because your highlighter touched every word.

Law school reading may seem daunting, but there is one major upside. Most law school reading assignments are shorter than college reading assignments. The trade-off however is that you have to read much more closely.

2. Step 2: Brief the Case

It's hard to read a case, understand it, and then be able to explain it to your professor while on call in front of the whole class. Most mortals struggle with these skills. And 1Ls are no different. Eventually, you will get very good at reading cases. And at some point in the future (probably when you're a 2L or a 3L), you will be able to simply read the case and then walk into class without notes and discuss it off the top of your head. It's a wonderful thing to look forward to. But that's in the future. As a 1L, you cannot just read a case and expect to be able to explain it to the professor when you are called on in class. You need to do more to prepare.

You should "brief the case" by preparing a short summary of the case. Case briefs should be short—less than a page. The purpose of briefing a case is twofold:

First, you are forcing yourself to explain the key aspects of the case. If you can't write a case brief, you are basically admitting to yourself that you don't understand it.

Second, a case brief will serve as a cheat sheet if you are called on in class. It will have the key information that a professor is likely to ask you about, so your turn with the Socratic Method will go smoother.

You have to write a case brief yourself. Don't use one from another student or from an online source. Writing the brief yourself is how you learn to analyze cases. Here's what goes in a brief:

1. The facts (but only the most important facts).
2. The procedural history. Which court is deciding this case and how did the case get here?

3. The legal issue that the court is deciding.
4. The holding—basically the legal rule and conclusion the court is adopting.
5. The rule—a principle from the case that can be applied to other cases.
6. The reasoning (the short version).
7. The outcome.

You should write out all seven of these items for each major case in the book. It will be tempting for you to skip the brief and just write these items in the margin of the textbook. Don't do that. Writing in the margin won't help you when you're on call because you won't have everything organized in one place. And, more importantly, taking notes in the margin doesn't force you to be sure you understand each of the seven items above. Writing a brief for each case takes discipline, but it is very much worth it.

3. Step 3: Think About the Case

As noted above, the standard advice for 1Ls is to read and brief cases before class. I'm going to ask you to go a step further though. After reading and briefing the case, I want you to take just a few quiet moments to ask yourself two simple questions. (1) How could the professor change the facts to make me think harder about the legal issues? and (2) Does the reasoning in this case make sense?

Let's brief a case so that you can see Steps 1, 2, and 3 in action. Below is a case about an attempted drug purchase that I teach in my Criminal Law course. As you'll see in the case, attempt crimes require the prosecution to show that the defendant wasn't just thinking about committing a crime. Instead, the evidence has to show that the defendant went further down the road. Attempt cases ask the question of whether the defendant "did enough" to have attempted the crime. Read the case below (it's interesting, I promise) and then we'll brief it on the other side.

United States v. Joyce

693 F.2d 838 (8th Cir. 1982)

Michael Dennis Joyce was convicted after a jury trial on one count of attempting to possess cocaine with the intent to distribute in violation of 21 U.S.C. §§ 841(a)(1) and 846 and one count of traveling in interstate commerce to facilitate an unlawful activity. . . For the reasons set forth herein, we reverse Joyce's conviction on each count.

I.

The facts as presented to the jury in this case are undisputed and based entirely upon the uncontradicted testimony of the government's only two witnesses: Robert Jones, a St. Louis police officer assigned to the Drug Enforcement Administration Task Force, and James Gebbie, a government informant.

During 1980, the St. Louis Metropolitan Police Department conducted what has been termed a "reverse sting operation," in which undercover police officers posed as drug sellers actively soliciting major drug transactions with reputed drug dealers. As part of that operation, government informant James Gebbie, who testified to having prior drug dealings with Joyce, contacted Joyce by telephone in September and early October, 1980, to inform Joyce about the prospective availability of drugs for purchase in St. Louis. Joyce told Gebbie to call back when Gebbie found out more definite information.

On October 20, 1980, Gebbie again called Joyce, this time informing Joyce that cocaine was available for purchase in St. Louis. Joyce indicated that he had twenty-two thousand dollars and would be in St. Louis the following day, October 21, 1980. Gebbie and

Joyce agreed that twenty-two thousand dollars would be more than sufficient to purchase a pound of cocaine.

On October 21, 1980, Joyce flew from Oklahoma City, Oklahoma to St. Louis, Missouri, where he met Gebbie and undercover officer Robert Jones, who was posing as a cocaine seller. Jones and Gebbie took Joyce to a room in a local St. Louis hotel, where Joyce immediately asked to see the cocaine. Jones told Joyce that the cocaine was not in the hotel room, but could be easily obtained by Jones if Joyce was interested in dealing rather than merely talking. After Joyce professed his interest in dealing, Jones recited prices for various quantities of cocaine and Joyce said that he could "handle" a pound of cocaine for twenty thousand dollars. Officer Jones then went to his office and obtained the cocaine.

When Officer Jones returned to the hotel room, he handed Joyce a duct-tape wrapped plastic package said to contain a kilogram of cocaine. Without unwrapping the tape, Joyce immediately returned the package, stating that he could not see the cocaine. Jones then unwrapped about half of the tape covering the plastic package and handed the package back to Joyce. Joyce again returned the package to Jones and asked Jones to open up the package so that Joyce could examine the cocaine more closely. Jones answered that he would only open the plastic package if and when Joyce showed the money that he intended to use to purchase the cocaine. Joyce then replied that he would not produce his money until Jones first opened up the plastic package. After Jones persisted in asking Joyce to produce his money, Joyce again refused, stating that he would not deal with Officer Jones no matter how good the cocaine was. Realizing that Joyce was not going to show his money or purchase the cocaine, Jones told Joyce to leave and Joyce left, with no apparent intention of returning at a later time to purchase any cocaine.

As Joyce left the hotel, he was arrested by DEA agents. A search warrant was thereafter obtained and used to search Joyce's luggage revealing twenty-two thousand dollars in cash.

II.

The issue before us is whether the evidence, taken in its entirety and viewed most favorably to the government, is sufficient to prove beyond a reasonable doubt that Joyce attempted to purchase cocaine with the intent to distribute. To resolve this issue we must determine whether Joyce's conduct crossed that shadowy line dividing acts of "mere preparation" to commit a crime and acts constituting an "attempt."

The government argues that Joyce's attempt to possess cocaine was established by evidence that he traveled from Oklahoma City to St. Louis with twenty-two thousand dollars pursuant to a previously discussed drug purchase arrangement, that he expressed an initial willingness to deal with Jones, and that he agreed with Jones on the price for a pound of cocaine. Furthermore, the government adds, Joyce would have purchased the cocaine had it not been for the disagreement between Joyce and Jones resulting from Jones' refusal to open the plastic bag containing the purported cocaine until Joyce first showed his money. The government points out that Jones was acting in compliance with DEA guidelines which prohibit illegal drugs from going into the physical possession of persons under investigation.

Joyce, on the other hand, contends that his conduct did not rise to the level of an attempt to possess cocaine because while he admittedly possessed sufficient money to purchase the cocaine at the agreed upon price, he ultimately refused either to purchase the cocaine or to produce his money. He thus had abandoned any designs he might have had of obtaining cocaine and distributing it before taking the necessary and overt steps of producing the money and obtaining the cocaine.

Although there is no comprehensive statutory definition of attempt in federal law, federal courts have rather uniformly adopted the standard set forth in Section 5.01 of the American Law Institute's Model Penal Code that the requisite elements of attempt are (1) an intent to engage in criminal conduct, and (2) conduct constituting a "substantial step" towards the commission of the substantive offense which strongly corroborates the actor's criminal intent. *United States v. Manley,* 632 F.2d 978, 987 (2nd Cir.1980). While we adopt this standard here, we are also mindful of Judge Learned Hand's candid, yet poignant, observation that a verbal formulation aimed at dividing mere preparation from attempt is, in itself, not particularly useful. Indeed, whether conduct represents a "substantial step" toward the commission of the criminal design is, in Justice Holmes' words, "a question of degree," necessarily depending on the factual circumstances peculiar to each case. *Commonwealth v. Peaslee,* 177 Mass. 267, 272, 59 N.E. 55, 56 (1901). However, as the Tenth Circuit analyzed in *United States v. Monholland,* 607 F.2d 1311, 1318 (10th Cir.1979):

> The cases universally hold that mere intention to commit a specified crime does not amount to an attempt. It is essential that the defendant, with the intent of committing the particular crime, do some overt act adapted to, approximating, and which in the ordinary and likely course of things will result in the commission of the particular crime.

With this in mind, we conclude that even assuming Joyce went to St. Louis intending to purchase cocaine, there was clearly insufficient evidence to establish that he engaged in conduct constituting a "substantial step" toward the commission of the crime of possession of cocaine with the intent to distribute. Whatever intention Joyce had to procure cocaine was abandoned prior to the commission of a necessary and substantial step to effectuate the purchase of cocaine. The attempt, of course, need not be successful, but generally the abortion of the attempt occurs because of events beyond the control of the attemptor. As the court recognized in *Monholland,* 607 F.2d 1319, "the [attemptor's] act must have passed the preparation stage so that if it is not interrupted extraneously, it will result in a crime." Here it is undisputed that Joyce, despite having both the opportunity and ability to purchase the cocaine at the agreed upon price, unambiguously refused either to produce his money or to purchase the cocaine. This effectively negated the government's effort to consummate the sale. . . .

The government, however, urges that Joyce's initially expressed interest in purchasing a pound of cocaine from Jones at the stated price and his momentary possession of the wrapped package said to contain a kilogram of cocaine constituted a substantial step toward possession of cocaine with the intent to distribute. We disagree. While Joyce professed a desire to purchase cocaine during his preliminary discussions with Jones, Joyce never attempted to carry through with that desire by producing the money necessary to purchase and hence ultimately possess the cocaine. And, although Jones gave Joyce the sealed and wrapped package said to contain a kilogram of cocaine, Joyce did not open the package but immediately returned the package to Jones who in turn refused to open the package because Joyce refused to produce the money necessary to effectuate the purchase of a pound of cocaine. Thus, all we have here is a preliminary discussion regarding the purchase of cocaine which broke down before Joyce had committed any "overt act adapted to, approximating, and which in the ordinary and likely course of things [would] result in the commission of the [crime of possessing cocaine with the intent to distribute]." *Monholland,* 607 F.2d 1318. . . .

Judgment reversed.

4. Example Brief

Now that we've read the case, let's brief it.

The Facts: Notice that the case has at least a full page of facts. Many cases will have even longer discussions of the facts. We don't want to re-copy a lot of facts though. Our goal should be to come up with a concise summary of the facts that provides only the crucial information needed to decide the case. Here's what I would say:

> *Joyce discussed buying $20,000 worth of cocaine from the informant. The next day, Joyce flew to Missouri and went to a hotel room to meet the informant and an undercover agent. Joyce asked to see the cocaine and said he could "handle" $20,000 worth. The under-cover officer then retrieved the cocaine and unwrapped it halfway after Joyce requested to see it. The officer asked to see Joyce's money, but Joyce would not show the money until the officer completely unwrapped the package (which the officer was not allowed to do under DEA rules). When the undercover officer asked to see Joyce's money, Joyce refused until the package was entirely unwrapped. Realizing the exchange would not happen, the officer asked Joyce to leave. The police later searched Joyce's luggage and found $22,000 in cash.*

Notice that my statement of facts is just a paragraph long. I have left out details that aren't relevant, such as the informant originally calling Joyce and then Joyce returning the phone call. Those facts might be relevant in an entrapment case, but Joyce never claimed entrapment so there is no reason to brief those facts. Finally, notice that I re-wrote the facts in my own words rather than cutting and pasting from the judicial opinion. It's important to be able to state things in your own words.

The Procedural History: Most cases you read will be appellate decisions. (Trial judges don't write many judicial opinions that you'll find in textbooks.) But it is not enough to know the name of the court that decided the case. You should also look for what happened in the court below (e.g. discovery motion, other pre-trial motion, jury trial, etc.). It may also help to know whether the case was in state court or federal court. (Here we know the case was in federal court because the statute in the first paragraph references crimes in the "U.S.C.," which is the United States Code. Here is how I would describe the procedural posture of the Joyce case:

A jury convicted Joyce in federal court of two crimes. Joyce has appealed to the Eighth Circuit Court of Appeals, which has issued the opinion we are reading.

The Issue: It is sometimes tricky to figure out the exact issue facing the court. One reason I picked this case for us to brief is that the court actually says "The issue before us is whether the evidence . . . is sufficient to prove beyond a reasonable doubt that Joyce attempted to purchase cocaine with the intent to distribute."

Even though a federal judge wrote this statement of the issue, it's not very good. It doesn't really tell you anything about the case. And we could use the same sentence for any other type of crime. So just because the court says something is "the issue" don't just take their word for it.

So what's the case really about? I think it is about whether the defendant committed the actus reus of the crime. And I think we determine that by assessing whether the defendant took a substantial step. So here is my issue statement:

Whether the defendant committed the actus reus of attempt by taking a substantial step toward the commission of purchasing drugs with the intent to distribute.

The Holding: The holding is the answer to the question you asked in your issue statement. You should state the court's decision, but go beyond simple phrases like "yes" or "no" or "reversed" or "affirmed." You want to answer the question raised in the issue with reference to the legal test. Here's what I think the holding is for the Joyce case:

> ***No, Joyce did not take a substantial step because even though he briefly held the drugs, he did not take any further steps that would be necessary to make his actions an attempt.***

The Rule: The rule is the principle you will draw out of the holding. It is a statement you can take with you and apply to another case. In other words, once Joyce's case is long gone, the Rule will be the principle that you can use in another case. (It's also the statement you will want to put in your outline down the road.) Here's the rule I draw out of the Joyce case:

> ***A substantial step (the actus reus of attempt) toward purchasing drugs requires more than simply traveling to a destination and holding the package of drugs.***

The Reasoning: The reasoning is your short description of why the court decided the case the way it did. In our case, the court seemed focused on what Joyce had left to do before he could complete the purchase of the drugs. What was left to do? Here's the court's reasoning:

> ***The court reasoned that Joyce did not take a substantial step because he had multiple steps left to take before he could have purchased the drugs. Specifically, he did not unwrap the package or produce the money that the seller demanded in exchange for the drugs.***

The Outcome: Often, the professor will open the discussion of a case by simply asking "What was the result?" Students (and sometimes even professors) can be very familiar with all the reasoning in a case but forget which way it came out. This is because the further into law school you get, the more you will recognize that the outcome of any particular case isn't actually that important. Your professor is not going to test you on which party won in a tort action between Smith and Jones. Instead, your professor will eventually test you on the rules you learned in that case. So you will learn to focus on the rules and will sometimes forget who even won the case. But you don't want to be called on in class and unable to answer a basic question like "What was the result in this case?" Therefore, it is helpful to just have a short phrase in your brief stating the outcome. So here's what I'd say for the outcome in the Joyce case.

The appellate court reversed Joyce's conviction.

If we put all of the pieces together, this is what our case brief will look like when we're all done:

United States v. Joyce

(8th Cir. 1982)

Facts:

Joyce discussed buying $20,000 worth of cocaine from the informant. The next day, Joyce flew to Missouri and went to a hotel room to meet the informant and an undercover agent. Joyce asked to see the cocaine and said he could "handle" $20,000 worth. The under-cover officer then retrieved the cocaine and unwrapped it halfway after Joyce requested to see it. The officer asked to see Joyce's money, but he would not show the money until the officer completely unwrapped the package (which the officer was not allowed to do under DEA rules). When the undercover officer asked *to see Joyce's money, Joyce refused until the package was entirely unwrapped. Realizing the exchange would not happen, the officer asked Joyce to leave. The police later searched Joyce's luggage and found $22,000 in cash.*

Procedural History:

A jury convicted Joyce in federal court of two crimes. Joyce has appealed to the Eight Circuit Court of Appeals, which has issued the opinion we are reading.

Issue:

Whether the defendant committed the actus reus of attempt by taking a substantial step toward the commission of purchasing drugs with the intent to distribute.

Holding:

No, Joyce did not take a substantial step because even though he briefly held the drugs, he did not take any further steps that would be necessary to make his actions an attempt.

Rule:

A substantial step (the actus reus of attempt) toward purchasing drugs requires more than simply traveling to a destination and holding the package of drugs.

Reasoning:

The court reasoned that Joyce did not take a substantial step because he had multiple steps left to take before he could have purchased the drugs. Specifically, he did not unwrap the package or produce the money that the seller demanded in exchange for the drugs.

Result:

Joyce's conviction was reversed by the appellate court.

Of course, your own brief might be longer. It takes practice to make a brief succinct, so don't worry if your initial briefs are longer. Remember, you are not turning in the brief for a grade, so don't worry about formatting and punctuation. The goal is to improve your class preparation and to force yourself to engage closely with the case. To that end, let's move on to Step 3 of your class preparation: "Thinking About the Case."

As you are "thinking about the case," remember to ask yourself two questions: (1) How could my professor change the facts to force me to think harder about the legal rules at play here? and (2) Is the professor going to challenge the reasoning of the case?

In terms of changing the facts, remember that the court in the *Joyce* case said there were two things the defendant had to do before completing the drug sale: (A) unwrap the drugs; and (B) produce the money. Your professor might ask the class "Would the court have decided the case differently if Joyce or the undercover officer had fully unwrapped the package of drugs?" If that happened, then the only step left would be for Joyce to produce the cash. Would it be more likely to be an attempt if there is only one thing left to do? Does it matter that the one thing is a really big thing? These are the questions your professor is going to ask, so it is worthwhile for you to at least start to think about them.

The second thing the professor will often do is question whether the court's reasoning makes sense. Magicians don't reveal their secrets. But, let's be honest, law professors aren't exactly magicians. So here's a secret from a textbook author: Sometimes, professors intentionally put cases in the textbook that are badly reasoned or wrongly decided. Why on earth would we do that? The reason is that when the professor discusses a court's incorrect reasoning it forces students to grapple with how a case should be analyzed. In other words, sometimes seeing how a case uses the wrong rule or how a case incorrectly applies the rule can help to show students what they actually should be doing instead.

Now, don't lose perspective. Most of the cases in your textbook will correctly state the law, and most cases will do a good job of applying that law. But sometimes, the courts mess up, and professors like to occasionally use those cases as a foil. Is the Joyce case one of them?

Well, the Joyce case definitely announces the correct rule for the actus reus of attempt. Most courts do in fact use the substantial step test. But announcing the rule isn't the only job a court has. The court also has to apply the rule correctly. Did the court apply the rule correctly in Joyce? I don't think so.

Notice that the court's reasoning is that Joyce never unwrapped the package and never produced the money. The court is right that Joyce had not in fact done those things. Those are steps that Joyce had not yet taken. But is that what the substantial step test asks courts to analyze? Nope. The test doesn't say you are guilty of attempt if there are no substantial steps left to be taken in the *future*. Instead, the test tells courts to look *backwards* to ask if you have already taken a substantial step.

So you might ask yourself "Has the court glossed over any substantial steps that Joyce already took?" Hmmm. I can think of a few:

- Joyce discussed the terms of a drug deal on the phone and said he could "handle" the amount of the drugs.
- Joyce then got on a plane the next day and flew to an entirely different state.
- When Joyce landed, he went to a pre-arranged meeting room in a hotel.

- While in the hotel room, Joyce further negotiated over the drug sale and actually held a partially unwrapped package of drugs.
- And to top it all off, Joyce brought $22,000 with him on the plane to another state.

Those things all seem like substantial steps to me. But let's use an analogy to confirm. Imagine you are in a serious long-distance relationship and your girlfriend has been talking about breaking it off unless you propose to her. You plead with her not to break up with you. You decide to take action. You call a jewelry store in Missouri where your girlfriend lives to start discussing buying an engagement ring. You then fly from your home in Oklahoma to Missouri where your girlfriend lives. You bring $22,000[1] in cash with you, to pay for the engagement ring. You then go to the jewelry store to further discuss the engagement ring purchase. You even hold the ring!

At that moment, your girlfriend calls and says she's breaking up with you because you couldn't be bothered to even take a substantial step toward trying to get engaged. Would you just agree with her and say "You're right. I didn't take a substantial step toward getting engaged." Or would you respond by saying "I've been negotiating with the jewelry store, I flew to your state, brought the money with me, went straight to the jewelry store, and I've even held the ring in my hands. Aren't those substantial steps?" I'm not sure about your girlfriend, but I would say "yes."

To be very clear, your professor does not expect you to think of the engagement ring analogy on your own before you've gone to class. I certainly wouldn't have been able to do it when I was a 1L. Additionally, you don't have to agree with me that the court reaches

---

[1] Extra points if you recognize that $22,000 would buy a really fancy engagement ring, especially in 1980!

the wrong result in *Joyce*. But you should begin to see that this is the type of discussion your professor will have with you in class. The court is not always right. And even if the court is right, there may be other arguments to consider that the court ignored. Your job in preparing for class is to start thinking about how your professor could change the facts or how your professor will push you to consider counterarguments that the court has ignored.

Points to Remember

- Read slowly and carefully. If you zone out or don't understand something, read it again.
- Write a case brief for each case in the reading (though not the tiny cases discussed in the notes section of the casebook).
- Resist the temptation to brief the case in the margin of your textbook. Scribbles you've written in the margin won't help you when you're on call.
- Try to keep your case brief under one page.
- Include only the relevant facts in the case brief. Write the facts in your own words and keep them short.
- Take the time to write out the procedural history, the issue, the holding, the rule, the reasoning, and the result.
- After you've written your brief, take a few minutes to think about the case.
- Ask yourself two questions after reading each case: (1) What facts could the professor change to force me to think harder about the legal rule? and (2) Does the court's reasoning make sense.

CHAPTER 10

The Socratic Method and the Classroom Experience

You're probably wondering "What is the classroom experience going to be like in law school?" And you're also probably wondering, "Is it going to be as scary as everyone says?" The short answer is that being in a law school class is much more demanding than being in an undergraduate class. But it doesn't have to be scary if you know what to expect and how to prepare for it.

Let's start with the basics. When you were in college, you probably took some large lecture classes and some small seminar courses. In the lecture classes, you probably just sat there and absorbed what the professor told you. The professor was there to give you information (and perhaps to entertain you) while you listened and typed it all down. In the seminar classes, the professor probably invited you and your classmates to share your opinions, perhaps too many opinions. Your 1L law school classes will not look much like your college lecture classes or your seminar classes. There will be less lecturing by the professor and less free form sharing of opinions. Instead, most law school classes are conducted with a version of the Socratic Method.

The Socratic method dates back to, well, Socrates and his conversations with Plato. The idea of the Socratic method is that the teacher asks a series of questions designed to guide the student to the answers. In the "pure" version of the Socratic Method (famously portrayed in the 1973 movie *The Paper Chase*) the professor never tells the students any of the answers. The professor simply asks question after question, and the class learns the legal doctrine from the students' answers to those questions.

The pure version of the Socratic Method was often a rough ride. Students frequently got the answer wrong, and the professor had no hesitation about letting the students know that they were wrong (which could be painful both for the person on call and the rest of the students who were rooting for him to succeed). And just when the student got close to the answer, the professor would "move the ball" by changing the facts in a way that would require a different or more nuanced legal analysis. After lots of wrong answers (and a few correct ones), the slow process of the Socratic Method eventually led to the right answer. Along the way, the controlling legal doctrines (hopefully) became clear to the rest of the class.

The core idea of the pure Socratic Method is that professors should never spoon-feed legal rules for the class to write down and later memorize. Professors who believed in the pure Socratic Method would tell you that anyone can look up answers in a book. Those professors didn't think they were training people to read the answers out of books. They were training lawyers. And lawyers are supposed to understand the logic of *why* the law works the way it does and to reason their way through the next case. In other words, the Socratic Method helps students learn how to reason through scenarios and apply the right rules in different situations.

The pure version of the Socratic Method sounds scary. The good news however is that few professors use the pure version of the Socratic Method anymore. Instead, professors use a limited (some might say, "softer") version of the Socratic Method. Your professor is likely to quiz you and your classmates about the facts of the case, the issue the court is deciding, the holding, and the reasoning. But long gone are the days when the professor refused to make any declarative statements telling the class what the law is. Most professors will acknowledge when the student has reached the correct legal rule. Indeed, many professors supplement the Socratic Method with some lecture during class sessions. In the old days, professors seemed to be most interested in frightening students, rather than teaching them. Those days are long gone though. Today, the Socratic Method is a teaching tool that professors use along with lectures, simulations, and practice questions.

Even though the Socratic Method is kinder today than decades ago, it can still be intimidating. To answer the professor's questions you need to (1) remember the key facts of the case; (2) identify the most important issues; (3) understand the holding of the case; and perhaps most importantly (4) be able to explain why the court chose a rule and whether its rationale makes sense.

Moreover, answering questions about the case you read is the easy part. Your professor is going to pivot (sometimes very quickly) to hypotheticals that were not in the case you read for class. Sometimes the professor will add, subtract, or change the facts of the assigned case. Other times, the professor will make up an entirely new hypothetical scenario. And the professor will expect you to take the principles from the assigned case and apply them to the new hypothetical she has dreamed up. And you'll have to do that on the fly, without time to think it over, and in front of the rest of the class. That's not easy to do!

So, to be perfectly honest, it's usually not all that much fun to be "on call" as a 1L student. But whether you're looking forward to it or not, it's going to happen. You can't escape it. So we should learn how to make the best of it. Being subjected to the Socratic Method doesn't have to be terrible. Here's how to make being called on less painful:

1. Read the assigned material carefully. As I said in Chapter 1, law school reading is shorter and denser than your college reading assignments. You have to not just read it, but read it slowly and carefully.

2. Write a case brief. After you have read the assigned material, the best way to be sure you can explain it to someone else is to be sure you can explain it to yourself. Writing a brief forces you to figure out the key facts, the issue, the legal rule, and the holding. Additionally, I don't know about you, but I forget details pretty quickly after reading them. Writing a brief is like writing a totally legal cheat sheet that you can bring with you to class. For tips on brief writing, see Chapter 9.

3. Pay attention throughout the entire class. Most 1L professors never announce in advance that they are going to call on you 15 minutes later. Nor should you expect that you'll only get called on at the start of a discussion. Sometimes professors switch mid-case from one student to another. And it's tough to answer questions when you didn't listen carefully to the answers that your classmate had been giving moments before. So you've got to pay attention.

   Let's pause on the issue of paying attention and be really honest with each other for a moment. I have to acknowledge that paying attention in class is harder for your generation than it was for mine. Back in my day, there was no Tik-Tok or Instagram. There are a million distractions on your laptop and cell phone that I never had to contend with. So I have sympathy when students get distracted in class. But I only have a little bit of sympathy. Professors still have a job to do. The Socratic Method only works effectively if students are paying attention. Your classmates (and your professor!) will get annoyed if the professor has to constantly repeat questions because you were shopping on Amazon or liking photos on Instagram. We can definitely tell the difference between a student who is taking notes and one who scrolling Tik Tok. There's a limit to how much zoning out a professor will tolerate.

Now it's time for you to be honest with yourself. Are you easily distracted by Tik-Tok, Instagram, and other applications on your phone and laptop? If you're human, the answer is probably yes. If the internet or your phone is going to distract you in class you need to shut it off. This goes double for Whatsapp or text chats. You will become friends with your classmates and will be very tempted to trade messages back and forth during class. Professors know students do this because we can see students on opposite sides of the room smiling at each other when nothing funny has happened in class.[1] The best advice for paying attention is to turn off any application that can distract you.

---

[1] I also know because I text with my professor friends during faculty meetings. Professors are human too.

4. If you haven't done the assigned reading and are unprepared for class, own up to it before class starts. Ask the professor not to call on you. Most professors are kind people. If you tell them you are sick or had a family emergency to deal with and didn't have time to read, most professors will let you "pass" on being called on. (To be sure, there are some tough customers who won't give you an inch, but they're rare.)

   While there is no harm in asking for a "pass" there are two obvious limitations on this advice. First, don't abuse your requests for a pass. It's not good for the professor to remember you as the person who repeatedly asks not to be called on. Second, asking for a pass only works if you do it before class starts. Don't think to yourself "Maybe I won't get called on, and so the professor will never know that I didn't prepare for class." If the professor calls on you and you only then confess to not having read, the professor is going to be annoyed and you're going to be embarrassed. So ask for a pass sparingly and in advance.

5. Don't make yourself a target for being called on. Everyone is going to get called on at some point, but the people who aggravate the professor get called on more often. It seems like simple advice, but it's important. Don't upset the professor. How do you avoid becoming a target of your professor's cold calls?

   - Don't be late to class.
   - Don't talk to the person sitting next to you while class is going on.

- Don't be visibly distracted. We can see if you are scrolling, surfing, or texting.
- Don't be disrespectful to the professor or your classmates when you speak in class.
- Don't be unprepared for class without giving your professor a heads up. When you're unprepared, the professor will come back to you in a future class "to give you another chance to redeem yourself."

So far I've given you the low-down on what the Socratic Method is and how to survive it. If you follow the tips above, you should do perfectly fine. Just for the sake of argument though, let's imagine that you get called on in class and that it goes badly. How should you react if you totally bomb a professor's cold call? I can offer advice from personal experience, because it definitely happened to me. Try to take this lesson to heart.

I was a shy 1L student. I rarely spoke in class and hoped ("prayed" might be the right word) that I would not be called on. I had ducked my Contracts professor for the first month of class, but eventually my time came. Before I tell you what happened, let me tell you a little bit about my Contracts professor. He never liked to tell anyone they were wrong. In fact, in the first month of law school, the professor never let the word "no" or "wrong" escape from his lips.

Instead of saying "no," my Contracts professor had three ways of responding to students. When a student was totally right about something, the professor would get excited and repeat the word "Right" four times in a row: "Right, right, right, right." When a student's answer was kind of correct (but partly wrong or off topic) the professor would also say "Right," but he'd say it twice and a little slower: "Riiiight, riiiight." And then if you were totally, completely wrong, the professor would also say the word "Right," but he'd say it only one time and very slowly: "Riiiiiiiiggghhhttttt."

Anyway, there we were, one month into Contracts and the professor finally called on me to ask me questions about one of the assigned cases. I'd read for class and written a case brief, so I was sitting pretty. I gave what I thought was a decent answer and I sat back waiting for my "Right, right, right, right" or at least "Riiight, riiight."

The professor didn't say "Right, right, right, right" though. Instead, he paused, looked at me and then said "No, actually that's not right." Then there was dead silence as students looked around the room. No one had ever been told "No" before in that class. The room felt kind of like when you watch a child fall down. The kid is definitely going to cry, but there is a delay while the child sucks in some air. After two seconds of silence, the kid loudly screams or cries. That was what happened in Contracts. Except I didn't cry (though it would have been perfectly reasonable under the circumstances). Instead, after the class sucked in air like a child that had fallen, there was a burst of laughter from the entire class.

Looking back on it, I don't think that the class was laughing at me. (Maybe I'm naïve, but I do truly believe this.) Instead, the class was laughing because the professor had finally said "No." And students found it funny because my bland answer—which definitely was not the craziest thing anyone had said that semester—was what finally made the professor say "No."

What's the moral of that story? Well, at the time I didn't see a moral to the story. It just sucked. I was definitely embarrassed. But there was a moral coming. And I hope you will indulge me because there is a point here besides my ego.

Even though I had the single most embarrassing moment on call in Contracts, I was the student who ended up with the highest grade in the class. Now, don't be too impressed. I didn't get the highest grade in any other class in law school. So I'm not telling you the story to brag about how great my grades were, because I certainly didn't graduate first in the class. I'm telling you this story for three totally different reasons:

First, no matter how badly you answer questions on call, it probably won't be as bad as how I did in Contracts. In fact, what you think of as doing "terribly" on call will not even phase your classmates. We are all likely to be much tougher on ourselves than our classmates would be in evaluating us. Put another way, people are bad at evaluating how they personally did on call in class. It is never as bad as it seems.

Second, if you actually do have an objectively bad day with the Socratic Method, it almost certainly doesn't matter. You and your classmates will be going to about a dozen class sessions per week for more than 3 months. That's upwards of 150 class sessions during your first semester. Trust me when I tell you that no one is going to remember how you answered questions in a single class session. Your classmates all have better things to do with their lives than spending time thinking about your performance in class that day.

Third, and most importantly, a bad day answering questions in class does not mean you are going to do badly on the exam. Law school is a race, not a sprint. And the race isn't won by smooth talking in class or seeming like a genius on call. The race is won by the hard work of reading the assigned material every day, paying attention in class, writing an outline, and studying hard.

Students who do well on call sometimes make the mistake of assuming they are ahead of the rest of the class. And students who are not as great on call often make the mistake of thinking they are behind and won't do well on the exam. After teaching law school classes for two decades and grading thousands of exams I can tell you that there is not always a big overlap between answering questions well in class and performing well on an exam.

So, don't let your self-worth and self-confidence be impacted by how you do when you're on call. Everyone has a bad day on call at some point. Just because you answer some questions wrong doesn't mean you're dumb or that you won't be a good lawyer. And the flip side is also true. If you kick butt on call, that doesn't make you a genius. Don't get arrogant. The race is long and you're not going to get an A on an exam in December just because you did a good job answering questions on a random Tuesday in September.

Instead, think of the Socratic Method as a means to an end. That's how your professors think of it. Professors are forcing you to struggle with lots of cases and hypotheticals because it makes you into a better critical thinker. You're in law school to *learn* how to think like a lawyer. So let the Socratic Method be a learning experience for you.

Points to Remember

- Law school professors usually use the Socratic Method. Your professor will ask you lots of questions and use your answers to elicit the legal doctrine the class needs to know.
- The Socratic Method is gentler than in the past. Your professor is not going to try to embarrass you. And the professor will likely supplement the Socratic Method with lectures and other exercises designed to teach you the material.
- The best way to prepare for the Socratic Method is to read carefully, write case briefs for each major case in the reading assignment, and to then carefully pay attention in class. Don't zone out when someone else is on call, because the professor could turn to you at any time.
- Tik Tok, Instagram, and everything else on the internet is distracting. Turn them all off while you are in class.

- If you didn't prepare for class, it's okay to occasionally ask the professor for a "pass." They may not give it to you, but there's no harm in asking. But you should ask sparingly and only before class. Don't wait until the professor calls on you to say you haven't read!
- To avoid the professor coming after you extra times, be on time for class, be prepared, don't talk to your seat neighbor, and be polite.
- None of your classmates are keeping score about how many questions you get wrong on call. It might feel like the whole world is watching you when you are on call, but everyone will forget 2 minutes later.
- You should expect to get things wrong when you're on call. Everyone does. You are not perfect. It's fine to make mistakes. In fact, wrong answers can help the professor to elicit the correct legal rules.
- If you mess up really badly on call it is not the end of the world. In most classes, your grade has nothing to do with how well you did on call. The race is long and doing well on the exam is your goal. Keep your eyes on the prize.
- If you do really well on call, don't get arrogant. Just because you are good at answering questions orally does not mean you will be good at writing an exam answer. Take your win in class and learn how to apply your skills to exam taking. Don't get cocky.

CHAPTER 11

Organizing the Takeaway Points After Class

Class is over for the week. What should you do next? First, take a little time for yourself. Go out with friends, read a book, binge a few episodes of whatever show you are watching. Reward yourself for completing a week of hard work.

After a short break, it's time to jump back in and start preparing for the next week. We know that preparing means reading the next assignment. But avoid the temptation to relentlessly march forward without looking backward. You don't learn just by reading the assignment and going to class. You also learn by reviewing the material you have already covered and by consolidating your thoughts.

So, first things first: Try to extract a few key themes and rules from each class session. Some class sessions may concentrate on a single rule. Other class sessions may be chalk full of rules. Your mileage may vary from class to class or subject to subject. But try to find the "takeaways" from each class session. And, of course, write down the takeaways. If it helps, you can color code the takeaways in yellow or some other color. Or you can just write the word "takeaways" and fill in some bullet points underneath it.

Now I know what you are thinking: "I don't need to write out takeaway points because I took notes in class, and I can review those notes later." That is not a good plan.

I don't say this to be discouraging, but let's just be very honest: Your class notes from the previous week are probably a mess. As you learned in Chapter 10, your professor will use the Socratic Method to force you to struggle with the legal concepts. As the class period goes on, you will write down lots of things that the professor and your classmates say. Some of those thoughts will be right, some will be wrong, some will be irrelevant, and many of them will be kind of messy as you type fast while trying to pay attention to what's coming next. Here's how this unfolds in class:

Imagine that the professor asks Student A about the facts of a case called *Summers v. Winters*. Student A starts to answer questions about the case, and you start writing down a summary of the case based on what Student A says in response to the professor's questions. But the professor seems not to agree with something Student A has said, so the professor moves to Student B. Student B then highlights different facts from the case and starts to explain the court's reasoning. Student B seems to be making sense, so you write down what Student B says and the next questions the professor asks. At some point though, the professor turns to yet another student. Student C agrees with Student B's discussion of the facts but focuses on a different line of reasoning from the court. You don't think Student C is correct, but the professor seems to be impressed with Student C's answers, so you think to yourself "Maybe I've missed the point. Maybe Student C has it correct." So you write down what Student C said and the professor's responses to Student C. After 15 minutes of this, you have written down a lot of stuff.

What you've done so far is perfectly normal. You're not 100% sure which of the three students is on the right track so you've written down everything. But notice that some of what you've taken notes on seems inconsistent. You've drawn a picture of the case, but it's not a very clear picture.

Eventually, the professor will signal what the right answers were. But the professor won't spoon-feed it to you. The professor will rarely say "This is the rule you should remember, and this is the reasoning that is correct." Instead, the professor may explain that Student A was right about the importance of some facts but that Student C had a better view of the reasoning. And the professor might say nothing about Student B (which might mean that Student B's comments were wrong, or irrelevant, or perhaps that they were mostly right but not phrased very well). Even if you type down the professor's comments, you still don't have a crystal clear statement of the rule and the court's reasoning. Instead, what you have is some language from the professor commenting on the rambling thoughts you've written down above.

Again, this scenario is totally normal. It's exactly what thousands of other students (including me) have written in their class notes since the beginning of time. But just because your class notes are normal does not mean that they are helpful. When you revisit your notes 3 weeks or 3 months later you are not going to understand what you wrote. You will not have a good idea of the rules and themes you should have taken away from that class session.

So you have to clean up your notes while the concepts are fresh in your mind. In an ideal world, it's best to clean up your notes and think about "takeaway" points right after every single class session. But let's also be realistic. You are in class all day and you have to read for tomorrow's classes. Most people are not going to have time to review and re-organize their class notes every single day of the week. If you can do that, great. But don't put that kind of pressure on yourself. Be realistic. If you can't review, revise, and consolidate your notes each day then do it every couple of days. And if you have to wait until the weekend when you have extra time, so be it. The key point is that soon after you've taken your class notes you should budget some time to re-read and re-write them into a cleaner format that you'll be able to use later.

Re-writing your notes is not the same thing as outlining. Outlining is a big undertaking. In Chapter 13, I describe in a lot of detail how to study for a law school exam and how to outline effectively. We're not up to that yet though. Summarizing your notes for the week is a smaller task that lets you ease into outlining later in the semester.

So what should you be doing at the end of each week? Here's an action list that consists of themes, rules, and cases:

1. Themes: Go through your class notes and try to write down the key themes of each class session. If you spent multiple days on a single topic, it's totally fine to consolidate those days together.

2. Rules: Try to write out clear statements of the rules you learned. Strip away all the student comments and half-transcribed questions from your professor that you've written down. Write a clear, crisp (and correct!) statement of the rules from each class.

3. Cases: When you eventually create an outline you will get rid of a lot of the discussion of individual cases. For now though, it's too early to do that. It is worthwhile though to shorten your description of each case to ensure you understand it. Read through everything you've written about a case and condense it. Include only the facts that mattered. Make sure

the reasoning is understandable and not just a bunch of half-written sentences that don't fit together.

Points to Remember

- As you take notes in class, you will end up writing down things that are irrelevant, unclear, or possibly even wrong.
- Shortly after each class session, you should go through your notes to re-read and revise what you have written.
- Don't wait until weeks later to review your notes because you will forget what you meant by some of the things you wrote down.
- When you review your notes look for key "takeaways" for each major concept. Takeaways include both larger themes and more specific rules.
- As you go through your notes you don't have to completely eliminate discussions of cases in order to focus on the rules. But you should shorten your discussion of each case so that it is succinct and easily digestible. You will use those abbreviated case notes when it is time to outline and study for the exam.

CHAPTER 12

Study Guides: What to Buy and What Not to Buy

One of the most common questions that students ask is "What study guides should I buy to help me do well on the exam?" Your professor may try to duck this question for two reasons. First, many professors think that if you read for class and pay attention all semester there's nothing else you need to read to do well on the exam. That advice may be correct for some students who just naturally "get" law school. But it isn't good advice for all students. Many people understand what the professor covers in individual class sessions, but they don't see the big picture of how all those cases and topics fit together. For those folks—which is probably most students—a study guide can really help to see the forest instead of just the trees. Moreover, almost everyone can benefit from doing practice questions that you'll find in some study guides. So I'm a fan of buying or borrowing *some* study guides.

The second reason why professors don't usually recommend study guides is that they don't read them. Professors are already experts in the subject area and don't usually need to read study guides to understand the law. Plus, there are a lot of study guides on the market, and your professor probably doesn't know which ones are better than the others. This is definitely true for me. I've taught Criminal Law for two decades, but I couldn't tell you which study guide is best. So, I can't tell you which specific books to buy for any of your 1L classes. But I can tell you what kinds of books are worth your time and money, and I can advise you on when to read them.

Before telling you which types of books to buy, let me offer a word of caution. There are a ton of law school study guides on the market. Some students feel better by purchasing a bunch of books. This just creates a false sense of security though. You can't learn a subject just by *owning* books on the topic. You actually have to *read* the books. (As I'll explain in Chapter 13, the same advice applies to studying in the library. Just being in the library has no intrinsic value by itself. For the library to be a valuable study space, you must actually study while you are there.)

The advice not to just buy lots of study guides probably seems incredibly obvious, but I regularly see students make the mistake of buying study guides just to feel better, but not actually read them. Study guides are expensive, so don't buy more than you need.

So let's figure out what you need. The first thing we need to do is understand the different types of study guides. So let's go on a tour of what's available.

1. **Case brief books:** These books track your specific casebook. Case brief books provide summaries of all the major cases in the textbook. In other words, case brief books are a cheat sheet that you can use when you are on call. They will tell you the key facts, the holding, the rule, and the reasoning for each major case in the book. In short, the case brief books will tell you the answers to some of the questions your professor will ask in class.

These books do the work for you. And not in a good way. A simple analogy would be going to the gym and then paying someone else to run on the treadmill for you while you sit in a chair and watch. You don't get the benefits of exercise if you're not the one doing it. The same is true for briefing cases and being subjected to the Socratic Method. The point of law school is for you to struggle with the material so that you learn the doctrine and learn to think like a lawyer. So, unless you are really, really struggling in class, I strongly advise you not to buy the case brief books. Do the work yourself. It will be worth it when you sit for the exam.

2. **Treatises:** These are big thick books that describe the law in intricate detail. Treatises are often called hornbooks (for reasons no one really remembers) or "green books" because the West Academic series of treatises have long had green covers. There are some fantastic treatises out there. For instance, I use the LaFave & Ohlin treatise to figure out difficult issues of Criminal Law. But treatises are really long—the LaFave & Ohlin book is nearly 1,500 pages—and they often focus on very complex and nuanced points of law. Treatises are way too detailed for a 1L. Don't buy these books, at least until you are a practicing lawyer.

3. **Overview books** (i.e. big-picture guides): There are books out there that show you the big-picture of a course. *The Short and Happy Guide* series (which includes this book!) is a good example. The overview books help you to see the major themes of a course and they highlight the most important doctrines. The

overview books will talk about some of the most important rules from your course, but they won't outline all of the key rules for you. These books are designed to show you the big picture and to help you understand the end-goals a professor is trying to reach. Plus, the overview books are usually fairly short and an easy read. If you liked Chapters 2 through 7 of this book about each of the 1L subjects, then you will find overview books useful.

4. **Outline books:** There are many study guides that go through each of the major topics and rules in a course. These books are often arranged in outline form (which is why I am calling them outline books). Outline books aren't focused on stepping back and showing you the big picture (the forest). They are more focused on detailing the blackletter law (the trees). Unlike treatises though, outline books give that blackletter law in manageable bites. Outline books will show you the most important rules you need to know. They do not get bogged down in every nuance and exception that you would find in a treatise. Instead, the outline books provide a basic narrative explanation of the key rules and then list those rules in an easily digestible format.

   The *Acing* series of study guides covers each 1L course by providing a checklist to follow. The *Gilbert* series does the same thing in more of a traditional outline format. There are lots of other books in this genre. One series is not necessarily better than the others. I personally like the *Acing* series, but your mileage may vary. It is a matter of personal preference on which format works best for you. Also, there are stronger and weaker books in each series. Ask upper-class students to recommend particular books for each particular class.

A word of caution though. While outline books can help you understand the legal rules, be careful not to over-rely on them. As I will explain in Chapter 13, it's important that you write your own outline in order to truly learn the rules you'll need to apply on the exam.

5. **Practice question books**: These books provide you with sample questions as well as model answers. Some practice question books are "objective," meaning they focus on multiple-choice questions with right and wrong answers. And some practice question books are "essays," which are fact-pattern questions with model answers. Obviously, if your professor is going to give an all-essay exam, then practice multiple-choice questions are less valuable. So check carefully what type of practice questions you are getting before you buy the book.

   As I explain in Chapter 13, it is incredibly valuable for 1L students to do practice questions to hone their exam-taking skills. So practice question books are very valuable. But a word to the wise: every professor teaches their course slightly differently. If you come across practice questions that address topics you did not cover in your 1L class, don't dwell on those questions. Do the practice questions that match what you covered during the semester.

So here is my general advice on what types of books to buy:

- Don't buy or use case briefs.

- Don't buy or spend time reading treatises.
- Do consider buying or borrowing an overview book.
- Do consider buying or borrowing an outline book.
- Do buy or borrow a practice question guide (unless your professor has made a lot of practice questions available).

If you decide to buy study-guide books, please don't buy too many. Specifically, don't buy multiple books from each category above. You don't need to read two or three overview books for a subject. You don't have time for that. If you buy an overview book and then hear that your classmate read a different overview book and loved it, you should resist the urge to go out and get another overview book. The same goes for outline books and practice question books. These books are *supplements*, not requirements. Don't go crazy with them.

At this point, I've told you what kinds of books to buy and that you should buy no more than one book per category. Let's go one step further and discuss *when* you should carve out time to read particular types of study-guide books. Here's my recommendation on the times in the semester when it makes more sense to read certain books:

1. Overview Books: Early Part of the Semester

If you buy an overview book, start reading it about three to four weeks into the semester. Why not at the very beginning? Because you likely have no idea what's going on during the first few weeks of classes. The first few weeks of the semester will be a blur, especially in your very first semester. Law school brings a new learning style, new friends, sometimes a new city, lots of reading, and a subject matter that is totally foreign. Give yourself a break and don't add too much extra in the first few weeks. On the other hand, it is useful to read an overview book before you have finished too much of the semester. An overview book will provide a great preview of the course and help you to start seeing the big picture. It never hurts to see that picture sooner rather than later.

2. Outline Books: Middle Part of the Semester

If you buy an outline book, start using it as a resource when you start outlining. As I describe in Chapter 13, you don't want to start outlining too soon. You really have to get about halfway into a course before you are in a position to start creating an outline. If you read an outline book too early, you will just have to read it again later when you are deep into your outline. So don't double your work. Wait until halfway through the semester to dig into an outline book.

3. Practice Question Books: Late Part of the Semester

If you buy a practice question book, wait until later in the semester to use it. There are two reasons for this. First, you can't take practice questions if your professor hasn't actually covered the material that's in the practice questions. Law school essay questions often test a lot of different concepts. If your professor hasn't gotten to some of those concepts yet, it's not going to help you to take a practice test about them. Second, even if you have covered the topics, you need additional time to review them. Just having read a few cases and attended a lecture about a topic doesn't mean you will know it well. Once you review the topic and outline that subject, you will be in a better position to take a practice test on the topic.

So you should wait until later in the semester to take practice questions. But don't wait until the very last minute to go through practice question books. You have multiple courses to study for and you might run out of time. So find the sweet spot. My advice would be about 2 or 3 weeks before the end of the semester.

4. Study Guides Are Supplements, Not Replacements

One final piece of advice: Do not—under any circumstances—let any type of study-guide book serve as a substitute for doing the assigned reading or paying attention in class. The professor may cover some topics that are not in your study guide. Or the study guide may devote a lot of time to topics that your professor doesn't think are important. And even when the topics completely overlap, your professor may see things differently from the author of the study guide. Law is not math. There is some subjectivity in how it is presented and analyzed. So your focus should be on the cases in your reading and your professor's discussion of them in class. Remember that study guides are a supplement, not a replacement.

The advice to use study guides as a *supplement* is particularly true for the outline books. If you buy or borrow a *Gilbert* book, an *Acing* book, or some comparable study guide that outlines the course for you, it will be tempting to just copy parts of the study guide instead of writing your own outline. That's a big mistake. As I explain in Chapter 13, it is very important to write your own outline. Writing an outline forces you to struggle with the concepts and to teach yourself anything you don't understand. It is totally fine to use an outline book to help you figure out the areas where you are confused. But don't give in to the temptation to just adopt the outline from a study guide. That's a recipe for not understanding the rules and not being able to apply them on your exams.

Points to Remember

- It's fine to ask your professor to recommend a study guide, but they may not have helpful recommendations. Professors don't usually read study guides.
- Case brief books are cheat sheets for when you are on call. Don't buy these. You can't get strong by paying someone else to exercise for you. Do your own work.
- Treatises are detailed explanations of the finer points of law. Treatises are great for lawyers, but 1Ls don't need them.
- Overview books explain the entire course at a high level. They are designed to show you the forest (and a few of the trees). It is often worth reading an overview book starting a few weeks into the semester.
- Outline books go topic by topic and set out the key rules and exceptions. Outline books can be useful to help you outline, but don't let them be a replacement for doing your own outline. And don't start using them before the middle of the semester.
- Practice question books are very valuable if your professor hasn't provided a lot of practice questions. Check the format of your professor's exam (essay or multiple-choice, or combination) and only get a study guide that matches that format. Don't dig into practice question books until later in the semester after you have covered the topics in the practice questions and had time to start reviewing what you learned all semester.

CHAPTER 13

How to *Prepare* for a Law School Exam: Outlining, Study Groups, and Practice Questions

Law school exams are entirely different from anything you will have experienced as an undergraduate student. In many classes—especially your 1L courses—the final exam counts for your entire grade (or at least most of it). Most law school exams are lengthy fact-pattern essays that require you to spot legal issues, figure out which topics are most important, and apply the legal doctrine you learned during the semester. Law school exams are usually time pressured and, let's be honest, they can be stressful. So how do you do well? You have to prepare the right way.

1. Step 1: Understand the Legal Doctrine by Outlining

To succeed on a law school exam you must understand both the high-level concepts and the specific legal doctrine. For instance, in Criminal Law, you need to understand that most crimes require mens rea to demonstrate the defendant's culpability. And you also have to understand the specific legal doctrines that separate a purposeful mens rea from other types of mens rea, such as recklessness. In other words, you need to see the forest from 30,000 feet, and you also need to see the trees up close.

How do you understand the big picture and the intricate legal doctrine? Obviously, you have to go to class and do the reading. But reading and attending class are not enough. Almost every first-year law student also makes an outline for each of their classes. An outline is an excellent way to learn and organize the complicated material you covered during the semester. But an outline only works if you do it effectively, so here's what you should do:

a. *Write Your Own Outline*

Let's start with the unpleasant part right off the bat. You should write the outline by yourself. Writing an outline is a lot of work. So you will be tempted to split the work amongst a few classmates so that you can save time. (You might even try to justify this to yourself by saying "if my friends and I split up the work we can each be more thorough in our own section of the outline and thus do a better job.") Here's some important advice though: Don't split up the outline. Write the whole thing yourself. Similarly, don't take the shortcut of buying a commercial outline and using that as all or part of your outline.

Why should you write your own outline from scratch by yourself? Because the act of writing an outline helps you to think carefully about the course material. It also gives you practice explaining—in writing—the most important legal principles, just as you will have to do on the exam. The best way to learn something is for you to personally struggle with it and write it down. Moreover, you don't need a perfect group outline that details every piece of information about the class in excruciating detail. Outlining is a dress-rehearsal for the exam. You aren't graded on the dress rehearsal. No one turns in their outline for a grade. The dress rehearsal (and thus the outline) only exist so that you will be prepared for the big day when you take the exam. The act of writing the outline is what will help you to perform well on the exam itself.

b. So How Do You Outline?

First, break the course into sections. The syllabus is a good guide for the structure of your outline. In Criminal Law for example, your outline should have big headings like Mens Rea, Murder, Manslaughter, Burglary, Insanity, Self-Defense, and other topics listed in the course syllabus.

c. Subject Headings and Holdings

Once you have major topics headings in place, organize your rules underneath these subject matter headings. For instance, in the mens rea section of your Criminal Law outline, you should have sub-sections about Purpose, Knowledge, Recklessness, and Negligence. And under each of those sub-sections, you should have rules that you learned during the semester that help you understand what behavior is purposeful as opposed to negligent. For each case you read or discussed in class, try to figure out the "holding." In other words find the key legal rule from the case and place it in the right spot in your outline.

d. Different Types of Rules

To successfully add the rules to your outline, you need to understand which type of rule you are dealing with. There are three main categories of rules: majority rules, exceptions to the majority rule for unusual situations, and minority rules.

Most of the cases you read during the semester will be about the "majority rule" that controls in most situations. The majority rules should therefore make up the bulk of your outline.

Majority rules are not the only thing to be concerned with though. You will read other cases throughout the semester that demonstrate "exceptions" to the majority rule. The exceptions are often relevant on law school exams, because professors love to test the nooks and crannies of a subject in order to separate the students who understand most of the material from the students who only understand some of the material. So as you outline you should clearly indicate what is a majority rule and right below that you should indicate any relevant exceptions.

Still other cases will introduce "minority rules" in which a state adopts a different rule from the majority approach. Be sure to clearly indicate in your outline when there is an important minority rule.

e. *Focus on Rules, Not Case Details*

When you write your outline it should be full of the rules that you have extracted from the cases you read, not the extraneous details from each case. Take a burglary case as an example.

Imagine that a court's decision begins by explaining that a couple got divorced a few years ago. When they got divorced, the ex-husband moved out of their home and the ex-wife stayed in the house. The ex-husband no longer has any ownership interest in the house. He shouldn't still have a key to the house. Yet, he does in fact still have the key. One day, the ex-husband had an explosive yelling match with his ex-wife in which they argued about what was best for their child. The court's decision details how the ex-husband screamed and threw things. The court then explains that at 11:00pm that night, the ex-husband used his key to sneak into the house with the intent to destroy some of his ex-wife's prized heirlooms. The case then spends a long time analyzing whether the ex-husband engaged in a "breaking," which is an element of the burglary statute. The court ultimately concluded that because the ex-husband should have surrendered the key when he moved out, his use of the key was a breaking.

There are a lot of facts in the paragraph above, but almost none of them should be included in your outline. For outlining purposes, you should not muddle your outline with details about the defendant screaming or throwing things. Nor does it matter what the defendant was yelling about, or even what time the ex-husband entered the house (because there is no debate about whether it was nighttime). The only thing that matters for your outline is the legal principle that using a key to enter can still be a breaking if the defendant has no permission to enter. Your outline should simply say something like "entering a house with the key can still be a breaking if the defendant was not lawfully entitled to possess the key."

To reiterate, a good law school outline focuses on the rules, not the very detailed facts of the cases you read. Don't just cut and paste text from your class notes. If your outline repeats lots of facts from the cases, it is not an outline of the rules but instead a bloated summary that will be hard to use.

f. *When to Begin Outlining?*

There is no perfect time, but generally it's smart to begin outlining halfway through the semester. I don't want to burst your bubble, but if you start too early in the semester, you will not really have any idea what you are doing. Law school is an entirely new way of thinking, and you will need a few weeks under your belt before you'll be in any position to start piecing together a picture of what you've learned. However, you should also remember that you have to outline for multiple courses (while still keeping up with your class reading). If you wait too long to start, you'll never finish. So don't start outlining too early, but don't wait too long either. Midway through the semester is usually a good strategy.

2. Step 2: Create a Skeleton Outline of Your Full Outline

Once you've written an outline, you'll have a long document that might be 20 or 30 pages long. Reading over that document is a great way to review for your exam. And your detailed outline will be useful during the exam to look up very specific points. But a long outline is not always helpful to glance through quickly when you're in the heat of battle taking a law school exam. It is therefore very helpful (and should be very simple) to also create a skeleton outline. A skeleton outline is a one-page reference guide that you can glance at as you are reading the essay question and writing your answer.

Why is a one-page skeleton outline helpful? The reason is that law school essay exams are "issue spotters." Lots of legal issues will be buried in a long fact pattern. As you begin to write about one of those issues, you will get very focused on that issue and will get lost in the details. In doing so, you may forget about other issues that you should address before moving on to a new part of the question. Having a one-page skeleton outline that you can easily glance at periodically will remind you about the issues to keep an eye out for.

Here's an example of how a skeleton outline can save the day: Imagine a Criminal Law essay question about two people—Amy and Betty—who rob a bank. The bank robbery was Amy's idea. She pitched the robbery to Betty, who agreed only to be the getaway driver. When the big day comes, Amy runs into the bank, pulls out a gun, and steals some money before getting caught on the way out. Both Amy and Betty get busted for the robbery. Naturally, as you are writing your answer you will spend time talking about Betty's role as an accomplice and what crimes she can be guilty of by assisting Amy. You will likely write a couple of paragraphs about Betty's accomplice role and when you're finished you may be ready to move on to the next question. But should you be done talking about Betty's criminal liability just because you discussed accomplice liability? If you look at your skeleton outline (which I've partly excerpted below), you might pause before moving on:

Skeleton Outline for Criminal Law

1. Murder—Intentional and reckless killings
2. Manslaughter—Heat of passion
3. Robbery—Using force or threat of force to take someone's property
4. Burglary—Breaking, entering, nighttime, felony inside
5. Accomplice Liability—Assisting and intending for principle to do the crime
6. Conspiracy—Agreement by at least two parties to commit a crime
7. Insanity—Understanding right from wrong vs. control test

Item 6 on your skeleton outline will hopefully jump out at you as you are scanning the list. If Amy and Betty made an agreement—indeed the facts above said that Betty "agreed"—they likely engaged in a conspiracy. And a conspiracy is a crime by itself (an important concept that you'll learn in your Criminal Law course). So you will want to write about Betty's liability not just as an accomplice but also as a conspirator. A skeleton outline will remind you to talk about conspiracy law, rather than just accomplice liability.

3. Step 3: Form a Study Group (if You Want), but Don't Overuse It

Lots of people form study groups in law school. A study group can be useful to discuss tricky issues and talk through concepts you covered in class that you did not understand. And, as I'll explain below, a study group can be useful to practice sample exams together. That said, study groups can become a problem, so follow these limitations:

1. Do not use the study group to split up writing your outline. Write. Your. Own. Outline.

2. Do not stick with a study group if it becomes a time suck. Some people "study" by just hanging out in the library and socializing. Just being in a library does not usually help anyone to learn the law. Of course, some down time is healthy. And having friends to talk and commiserate with is *very* valuable. But don't pretend that your social time is study time. If you find your study time is mostly socializing and not studying, then you will need to limit how much time you spend with the study group or perhaps leave it entirely.

3. Do not get involved with a study group that creates drama. Students will sometimes say that law school can be a little like high school. Law schools are usually smaller than colleges and often have about as many students as high school did. Classes are typically all in the same building. You see the same students repeatedly in classes and in the hallways. And most students are single and in their 20's. Sometimes, drama ensues. And that drama can be draining both in terms of time and emotional energy.

> The most valuable commodity in law school is your time and your clear mind. Don't spend your emotional energy on other people's drama. If your study group is causing you headaches, get out.

4. Step 4: Take Practice Exams the Right Way

Law school exams are only partly about knowing the rules. They are also about deciding which issues are most important and explaining clearly how courts should decide them. In other words, law school exams are not a statistics question in which the answer is either right or wrong. The organization and coherence of your answer matters a lot on law school exams.

You've probably never seen anything like a law school exam as an undergraduate, so it's very important to practice for them in advance. Your professor may make old exams available. If so, you should take every one of them exactly as you would if it were a real exam. If there are time limits or word limits on the practice exam, you should follow them exactly. It's also a good idea to find other practice exams—either from a study guide or from another professor's old exams—and take those sample exams as well.

In taking practice exams, there are two things you should absolutely do, and one thing you should definitely not do.

- *Do* write out the entire answer as if you were taking a real exam.
- *Do* find a study partner who will also take the same sample exam and share their answer with you.
- *Don't* look at the model answer or discuss the question with classmates before you take the sample exam yourself.

Here is why you should follow these "do's" and "don'ts."

A law school exam does not actually test how much law you know. A law school exam tests how much law you can convey to the professor in a clear and organized fashion. What is in your head is not always the same as what you end up typing on the screen. Students often *think* they have written down the rules, the relevant facts, and their conclusions, but they do not always actually type them down. In other words, as they are taking the exam, some students think of the right analysis in their heads, but they do not actually type it down and thus cannot get credit for it.

This is why it is important to write out the entire answer to practice essay questions. When you write the entire answer out you can re-read your answer and see whether you have in fact hit the important issues and correctly described the law. You can also see what your classmate has written and what issues they spotted and discussed. When you read a classmate's exam answer, the odds are you will have an epiphany and say something like "Well, I knew all the law that my classmate referenced, but I just didn't write it down." The trick for a law school exam is to get the information from your head onto the page. Writing out a complete answer to a practice exam can help you see what topics you need to spend more time studying. If you just think about the answer in your head, you might convince yourself that you know how to talk about the topic. But actually writing it down, step-by-step, might reveal that you get stuck on how to explain one part of the analysis.

Practice exams also serve to improve your writing. Law school exams are not just about hitting the right issues and stating the law correctly. Professors also want to see that you have organized your exam answer clearly. If you speed through a practice exam only to see whether you have gotten the answer right or wrong, you will not notice areas where your writing and organization need improvement. For instance, you can correctly conclude that something is an Equal Protection violation without clearly stating the test, which facts are controlling, and why those facts matter. But if you write down your practice exam answer, force yourself to read your answer, and also see how another student organized her answer, you will quickly get a sense of whether your answer was well written and well organized.

The same logic explains why you should ***never***—notice the bold font, ***never***—read the model answer or talk about the exam question with a classmate before you have actually taken the practice exam. If you glance at the model answer or discuss the question, you will never know how you would have answered the questions if you took the exam completely cold.

I'll repeat myself because this is important. You don't just want to practice for your exam, you want to practice correctly. And that means taking lots of sample exams, answering them just as you would if it were a real exam, and only then talking with a classmate and exchanging your answers.

Finally (and this is hard because you will be tired by now), wait a few days and take the same practice exam a second time. Once you've seen the parts of an essay question that you missed or that you could have explained better, don't just say to yourself "Now, I get it." Go one step further and force yourself to re-write the answer. Re-writing your answer will push you to phrase things more clearly and more completely the second time.

5. Step 5: Maintain Balance in Life, Even During Exam Season

As we've discussed earlier, law school is time-consuming and can be stressful. It is important to take care of your physical and mental health. Get outside. Exercise. Go out with friends. Do things you enjoy. And definitely try to eat well and get enough sleep.

You can only study so much before you become exhausted. And if you're exhausted you won't perform well on your exams. Remember, no one is grading your outline or how many hours you spent studying. Be rested and in a good state of mind for your exams. So quit studying at a reasonable hour on the night before an exam. A healthy meal and a good night's sleep will serve you better than staring at a textbook for a few more hours.

Points To Remember

- Write your own outline, starting around the middle of the semester.
- Focus your outline on rules—the majority rules, exceptions, and minority rules. Don't get bogged down in the facts of the cases you read.
- Create a skeleton outline to help with issue spotting.
- Take lots of practice exams. Answer the whole question in the time allotted and don't look at the model answers or discuss the questions with classmates before you've fully answered the questions yourself.
- After you've taken practice exams, exchange your answers with a classmate so that you can see how other people answered the same question.
- Form a study group if it works for you. But remember that sitting with a group in the library is not always the same thing as studying.
- Maintain balance, even during exam season. Remember to eat well and sleep enough.

CHAPTER 14

How to *Take* a Law School Exam

Lots of people are going to offer you advice on how to do well on your law school exams. You may have friends or relatives who are already lawyers and thus think of themselves as experts on exam taking. You may also have friends who are 2Ls and 3Ls who think they have figured it all out already. Their advice may be good, or it may be terrible, depending on who you talk to. But either way, it's probably going to be pretty generic and amorphous. So my goal in this chapter is to offer you 10 concrete tips for performing well on your law school exams.

These 10 tips are based on having graded thousands of exams over the last two decades. Once you've read enough great exam answers and enough lousy ones, you develop a strong sense of what students are doing right and what they are doing wrong. These 10 tips aim to put you on the right track.

Perhaps most importantly, I use the last tip in this chapter to show you a good essay answer and a bad essay answer. These answers don't come from real students—I wrote them myself. But they look like thousands of other good and bad answers I've graded over the years. Without further ado, let's get started.

1. Be Prepared

Tip #1 is the simplest, but the most time consuming. You have to be prepared for class in order to digest the complicated material your professor is covering. In other words, you cannot perform well on an exam unless you have learned the law that is covered on the exam.

It's impossible to be prepared for an exam if you have not been keeping up with the reading and paying attention in class all semester. Don't skip reading assignments or blow off classes. Even if you have a hard time following your professor or are frustrated by how dense the reading is, you have to keep reading the textbook and going to class.

As I explained in detail in Chapter 13, you should make an outline for each of your doctrinal courses. Write your own outline. And then make a one-page skeleton outline that hits all the high points.

Toward the end of the semester, take as many practice exams as you can. Do the practice exams as if they were real. Don't look at the answer key or talk with your classmates until after you have taken the exam. Once you've finished taking a practice exam, you should definitely compare answers with a classmate and debrief what you could each do better.

Being prepared is not just about studying. Maintain balance and mental health during exam season. If there is something you enjoy doing (running, knitting, playing guitar, or whatever else), it is really important that you keep doing it.

As the exam approaches, you should also remember more mundane matters. Make sure your laptop is in good shape. If your law school has exam software and gives you an opportunity to try it out in advance, take the opportunity to do a dry run. You should also ensure that you have enough of your favorite snacks and drinks to get you through the exam.

Finally, being prepared includes having a plan for getting to the exam on time. Budget extra time. Get to the classroom early. You don't want to waste dozens of hours studying by being frazzled as the exam starts.

2. Know That It's Okay to Be Nervous

The odds are that you will be nervous in the days and moments before an exam, especially for your first law school exam. There's no magic way to get rid of nerves, but here are some things to make you feel better about it.

Most people get nervous before exams. Even the people who look calm and collected on the outside are probably super nervous on the inside. The mistake that law students often make is to assume that everyone else is in better shape than they are. It's almost never true. The odds are that the rest of your classmates are nervous too.

Finally, being nervous is not all bad. Being nervous can make you focused.

Bottom line: As you walk into an exam. Don't freak out about being freaked out. Everyone else is in the same boat as you. And if your classmates say they're not nervous, they're probably lying.

3. Read the Exam Question Twice and Circle the Call of the Question

Once you crack open the exam, you will be faced with a lot of words to read. Law school essay questions are usually at least a page of full text. Many exam questions are much longer, sometimes upwards of five pages of dense reading. When you open the exam and see a ton of text to read, what should you do?

First, go to the end of the question and find the "call of the question." In other words, look for the line that tells you what the question is asking. In Criminal Law, the call of the question might ask you what a defendant can be charged with and what defenses he can assert. In Torts, it might ask what a defendant can be held liable for. In Contracts, it might ask about whether a contract has been formed, whether it has been breached, or what the damages might be. Having a sense in the back of your mind of what you are being asked to do will help you as you start to read the question. You don't want to start the exam by focusing on irrelevant things that are not the actual question you will have to answer. You want to immediately start getting in the zone for your answer.

Second, read the question. Full stop. Just read the question. Don't start writing anything. I'll say it again. Start by just reading the question. Students are often tempted to start writing as soon as they see an issue they know something about. Worse yet, when you hear another student's keyboard start clicking you will feel like you are falling behind, and you will feel pressure to start typing to keep up. Resist the urge to start typing before you have read the question completely.

Third, and this is really hard to make yourself do when you hear other people typing, read the question a second time. As you read the question the second time, it is okay to start underlining and taking notes. If you absolutely have to start typing something, limit yourself to writing out headings, a topic we'll come to now in Tip #4.

4. Outline Your Answer Using Headings

This chapter includes ten tips for doing well on law school exams. Here's how I wrote this chapter. First, I wrote down all ten tips. If you looked at the page as I was starting to write this chapter, all you would have seen was a list of the ten tips with no text written underneath any of the headings. Only after getting all ten tips down on paper did I go back and fill in an explanation for each one.

Why did I list the key topics first and only then go back and fill in the details? Because I don't have an exceptional memory, and I probably would have forgotten some of my ideas if I hadn't written them down as soon as I thought of them. If you have an exceptional memory, you can ignore Tip #4. But guess what? Almost no one has an exceptional memory. Most people have average memories, and that can be a problem for law school exams. Here's why:

Recall that a law school essay question is multiple pages long. Buried in those pages are lots of issues you will need to spot and lots of facts that will help you to stake out a position on those issues. As you are reading the question, the issues and facts will start popping out at you like fireworks on the 4th of July. For instance, your Criminal Law exam might have a burglary question on it. (And as you may recall from Chapter 3, burglary is usually defined as breaking and entering the dwelling house of another at night with the intent to commit a felony inside.) As you are reading the question, you might see that the back door of a house was open and that only a flimsy curtain stood between the defendant and the inside of the house. The professor put that issue there to see if you understand what a breaking is. Later in that same paragraph, the question mentions that the crime happened at 11:00pm in April in Illinois. Here the professor is checking to see if you spot the issue of whether it is nighttime.

As I was reading the exam question the second time, I would type down the following two headings and nothing else:

Walking Through a Curtain Can Be a Breaking

The Entrance Occurred at Nighttime

I would not write out an answer under either heading. Instead, I would keep reading though the rest of the essay question and I would keep listing headings like those above before writing a word of explanatory text. Why do I recommend writing all the headings first? Because you will likely forget some of the later issues if you immediately start explaining the first issue you see. Let's see how this can easily happen:

As you think about the curtain standing between the defendant and the inside of the house, you will likely start to explain that a curtain is not a door. It does not require that you use a key or turn a handle. An animal without opposable thumbs can get past a curtain. You would therefore probably write about how a curtain doesn't really block anyone or anything from entering. On the other hand, you might also explain how the defendant would have to physically move a curtain to one side to get into the house. This seems a little like opening a door or pushing up an unlocked window, which you may have talked about in class as qualifying as a breaking.

By the time you are done with analyzing the curtain, you will probably have taken a couple of minutes to write a full paragraph. What comes next? Well, if you have a good memory, you will recall that the question also mentioned that it was 11:00pm in April in Illinois. So you might remember to write about the "nighttime" issue. But it's now been a couple of minutes since you read that paragraph of the exam question. And after writing about the curtain for a few minutes you may well have forgotten about the time of day. If that happens, you will completely skip over the nighttime question and instead move on to the next paragraph of the fact pattern.

If you write absolutely nothing about the nighttime issue you will get zero points for that issue. Most professors will give you points just for spotting an issue. Indeed, professors will usually give you some points for analysis that is in the ballpark, even if your analysis isn't what the professor was looking for. So it is a huge mistake on a law school exam is to skip an issue, especially an easy issue. It is therefore crucial that you find a way to hit all the issues that you spotted when you read the exam question initially.

The main benefit of writing headings for each issue is that it prevents you from entirely skipping issues. Once you have written down a heading for an issue it is there on your screen and will not disappear. Even if you never write another word about it, you will have spotted the issue and may get at least a few points for it.

A secondary benefit of writing headings is that they help to organize your answers. Headings will help keep your analysis in order. It will subdivide your answer so that you can see which parts of a topic you've addressed in depth, compared to which topics you've skated by quickly.

A third benefit of headings is that they help your professor to read your answer and see that you spotted issues and addressed them. Most professors read every word of every exam answer. We take our jobs seriously and are very careful as we grade. That said, professors are human. We are often reading dozens upon dozens of answers about the exact same question. We get tired and inadvertently lose focus. It is much easier for professors to see what you have written when it is divided in small, easily digestible pieces. Which in turn leads us to Tip #5.

5. Use Sentences and Paragraphs, Not Bullet Points

Law school exams are usually time pressured. As a result, you will be in a rush to write down what you know. This creates a temptation to write quickly and sloppily. Worse yet, time pressure leads some students to write their answers in bullet points or sentence fragments. This may make it more difficult for your professor to figure out what you are trying to say. You need to write in complete sentences that are separated into paragraphs.

I could explain the value of writing in clear sentences and organizing those sentences into paragraphs. But you already know this, so I won't belabor it. I'll just add that professors are grading the coherence of your legal analysis. And you will seem a whole lot more coherent if you write in clear sentences and paragraphs.

How do you write coherently? Practice. You will hone your writing skills in your Legal Research and Writing course. Additionally, you can further enhance your writing by following the advice in Chapter 13: Take a lot of practice exams; actually write out your answers; and then re-write your answers after going over them with a classmate.

In short, many students come into law school without having done a lot of writing as undergraduate students. And law schools put a lot of emphasis on clear writing. The best plan is to assume you are not a good writer and to practice as much as you can before your exams.

Clear writing is important and you should put efforts into being clear as you write your exams. But there are two caveats (which I hope don't undermine the importance of what I have said above).

First, you are not publishing your exam answer. The writing cannot be perfect when you are working under major time pressure. Your job is to be as clear as possible while still getting through the substance of your answers. In other words, spend time fixing the clarity of your writing, but don't spend *too much* time. Unless a professor has told you that she cares about case names being italicized, don't worry about cosmetic things like that. Try to write clearly and accept that it won't be perfect.

Second, the rules of the game change if you are coming to the end of time on an exam and still have more to say. If you have only a couple of minutes left and lack the time to write clear sentences and paragraphs about a final topic or two, don't just give up. At this point, you should use bullet points or even sentence fragments to put down any issues and analysis you can. Some professors will be sticklers and won't give you points for incomplete thoughts at the end of an exam. But other professors will give partial credit if you can show you know something about an issue but ran out of time.

6. State the Rule Clearly

Law school exams test your ability to spot rules and apply them to the facts in the exam question. We'll cover how to deal with the "facts" in the next tip, but for now let's figure out how to handle the rules.

To state the obvious out the outset, identifying and correctly stating the rules shows the instructor that you've learned the course material. And most instructors give points on an exam just for spotting and stating the rule. So, when in doubt, it is always a good idea to very explicitly state the rule.

Stating the rule sounds obvious, but students mess that up by skipping to the application of the rule too quickly. For instance, in our burglary hypothetical, students will sometimes quickly say something like this:

> "Defendant cannot be convicted of burglary because it was too early in the day for that crime to have occurred."

Nothing in that statement is wrong, but it's incomplete. The professor can guess that you understand the rule. But it's not totally clear that you are saying the element of nighttime is required. So, odds are, you are not going to get the maximum number of points for this answer. It would be better for you to instead write the following:

> "The burglary statute requires that the actions occur during the 'nighttime.' If the defendant broke and entered during the daytime, it could still be a crime, but that crime would not be burglary."

The bottom line is that you should double-check that you are actually stating the rule.

7. Mention the Most Important Facts, and Use the Word "Because"

The difference between an average exam answer and an excellent answer is often how well the student references the facts and then uses the word "because" to tie those facts to a conclusion. When you spot an issue and tell the professor the rule, you also need to explain why that issue and rule matter. And to do that, you typically need to mention the most important facts and make logical deductions. The best answers tie together the rule, the facts, and then reach a conclusion. The word "because" is often your best friend because it forces you to wrestle with the rule and the facts and reach a conclusion.

Let's take our "nighttime" burglary problem again. Recall our rule from Tip #6 above:

> "The burglary statute requires that the actions occur during the 'nighttime.' If the defendant broke and entered during the daytime, it could still be a crime, but that crime would not be burglary."

Some students will write a perfect rule statement and then stop there. That is not enough though. You have to also draw the key facts out of the exam question. It is therefore crucial that you follow the rule by adding the part in italics:

> "The burglary statute requires that the actions occur during the 'nighttime.' If the defendant broke and entered during the daytime, it could still be a crime, but that crime would not be burglary. *The fact pattern tells us that the breaking and entering occurred at 11:00 pm in the month of April in Illinois. Because 11:00 pm is nighttime, that element is satisfied."*

Our answer is now much better because we have stated the rule and located the controlling facts from the exam question. The nighttime element of burglary is satisfied *because* it is dark at 11:00pm in April in Illinois and everyone agrees that it would be nighttime that late in the evening.

8. Make Logical Inferences and Assume Facts, When Appropriate

One of the hardest parts of a law school exam is knowing when it is okay to add facts and assumptions that are not in the fact pattern. This is art and not science. But let's try to create some guideposts.

First and foremost, do not change the basic facts of the exam question. In our burglary hypothetical, the question says that it is 11:00 pm in Illinois. Do not change those facts to say something like "Well, if it were 6:00 pm it might not be nighttime." Similarly, don't say "if it were 11:00 pm in the summer Alaska when it is light out all day then it would not be nighttime." The question specifically says it is 11:00pm in Illinois and you have to roll with that. Similarly on your Torts exam, if the professor tells you that a child was attacked by chihuahua (a tiny dog), don't change the facts and analyze whether the answer would be different if the dog were a rottweiler (a large aggressive dog). Professors choose the facts for the exam, and they don't like it when you change them.

On the other hand, there are times when it is okay to assume facts or consider how the "blanks" should be filled in. Let's take the nighttime issue from our burglary question once more. Instead of the exam saying it was "11:00 pm in Illinois in April" imagine that the exam said that it was "7:00 pm" and offered no further information about the location or the time of year. In other words, imagine that the professor wrote ("It was 7:00 pm." Full stop.)

Now it would be okay to expand the facts in the hypothetical to demonstrate your fluency with the nighttime issue. For instance, your answer could say something like the following:

> "The burglary statute requires that the actions occur during the 'nighttime.' If the defendant broke and entered during the daytime, it could still be a crime, but that crime would not be burglary. The fact pattern only tells us that the breaking and entering occurred at 7:00pm. That might be at nighttime, but we would need more information to know for sure. For instance, what time of year is it? It stays lighter much later in the summer months than in the winter months. Additionally, it would be helpful to know where the breaking and entering took place. In the summertime, it stays light much longer in the northern states than in the southern states. Thus, if it were 7:00pm in the month of May it might be light in Minnesota but dark in Florida. The bottom line is that it is unclear from the facts whether it is nighttime and whether that element of the burglary statute can be satisfied.

Professors sometimes leave important facts out of the question on purpose to see who will notice and analyze them. And, let's be honest, sometimes professors leave out important facts by accident. Either way, it is useful to add facts when doing so helps to fill in gaps that normal people would want to know about. But don't change crystal clear facts.

9. Focus on the Most Important Issues, Which Are Usually the Debatable Issues

Another huge challenge on a law school exam is deciding what to devote your time to. Professors obviously test whether you know the rules and can apply them. But they are also testing whether you can figure out which rules are the more important in a particular situation and thus most deserving of more detail in your answer.

As you already know, the average law school exam is a lengthy essay question that sets out a ton of facts and then says something like: Explain the crimes the defendant could be charged with and the strength of those charges. Or the call of the question might be even more vague and say: Explain all the Contracts (or Property, or Torts) issues that are important and whether the plaintiff is likely to prevail. In other words, the professor will give you a long set of facts, an open-ended question, and multiple hours to write an answer with almost no guidance on what to say. Or a professor could impose a word limit, leaving you to decide whether you should spend 100 words or 1,000 words writing about one Property law concept as opposed to another.

With multiple hours to write and a ton of topics that you could cover it's your job to decide which topics deserve a lot of your attention and which can be dealt with quickly. How do you do that?

In some cases, professors are kind enough to recommend how long you should spend on each part of a question. If you are offered that gift, please take it. I have repeatedly seen students spend an hour on a question that is allocated 30 minutes of time. When they do that, you can imagine what happens next. Those students run out of time and don't finish the questions that come afterwards. And if you run out of time you will miss all the points for those issues, even the easy points that you surely would have gotten. So, if a professor gives you a specific number of minutes to spend on a question you should follow their recommendation.

Unfortunately, your professor might not tell you how long to spend on each part of a question. They want to see if you can figure it out. So how do you know? The honest truth—unfortunately—is that you have to understand which issues the professor thinks are most important and deserving of the most time.

For some professors, a good rule of thumb is to think about whether you spent a lot of time on an issue in class. If the professor talked about the topic for 15 minutes over the course of the entire semester, they usually will not make that topic a huge part of the exam. As a result, you should probably not write a ton about a topic you barely covered in class. This is a rule of thumb though, not a rule written in stone. Some professors can be tricky (or idiosyncratic, or maybe a little grouchy), so you have to use this rule of thumb cautiously.

Another way to approach the problem is to ask, "How important is this issue to determining whether the defendant wins or loses the case in the fact pattern?" If an issue seems "dispositive" it's probably something you'll want to spend a bunch of time on. But even that can be deceiving. Sometimes a dispositive issue is really simple. So while it's a good rule of thumb to focus on the issue that may win the case, don't follow that guidance if it leaves you with little to write about.

Instead, the single most important guideline is that you should devote a lot of time to issues that are debatable. Because this is so important, I have made Tip #10 (below) an explanation of how to answer a question when the issue is debatable. But before explaining how to answer a debatable issue, let me first say how you determine whether an issue is even debatable in the first place and thus deserving of a lot of your time on the exam.

Let's take our burglary hypothetical one more time:

> At 11:00 pm somewhere in Illinois, a defendant goes to a house where the front door is open. To get inside, the defendant has to move away a cloth curtain and walk in through the open door behind the curtain.

The nighttime issue is not the slightest bit debatable. Maybe if it were Alaska in the heart of summer when it could be light at 11:00 pm it would be debatable, but not in Illinois. This issue is not deserving of more than a sentence or two.

By contrast, the curtain raises a debatable issue. You cannot commit burglary unless you engage in a "breaking." And as you'll learn in your Criminal Law course, you create a breaking by making an opening where one did not previously exist. Does moving aside a curtain count? I think the answer is "yes" but I would not limit my answer to saying that "moving aside the curtain is a breaking." Rather, I would first explain the rule that a breaking is required. And I would then say that courts have decided that walking through an open door is not a breaking. And then I'd contrast that by explaining that pushing open a window or twisting the handle of a closed but unlocked door has been found to be a breaking. So if the defendant had to push aside the curtain with his hands that would seem like a breaking.

On the other hand, what if the defendant entered by sliding his body around the curtain? Perhaps he didn't even touch the curtain, or maybe he barely brushed against it in order to enter. I'd argue that such behavior looks quite different than manipulating a door handle or using physical force to push open a window. In other words, even though I think pushing aside (or moving around) a curtain is a breaking, the issue is debatable. And debatable issues are what professors want you to focus your answer on. Look for issues like the curtain, where you have to apply the cases and concepts you learned during the semester and where the answers could come out differently depending on which cases you rely on.

Given that debatable issues are the main event, let's figure out how to *answer* those types of questions.

10. Consider Both Sides of the Issue and Then Take a Position

Some professors ask essay questions that have lots of clear right answers. Those professors are pretty unusual though. Most instructors think law school is supposed to train sophisticated thinkers. As a result, most professors think exam questions should be more complicated than having simple right or wrong answers. Most exam questions therefore test debatable questions where you have to state the rule, build an argument, and then take a position on which side of the argument is better. For these exam questions, the answer will be debatable and there will be facts in the question that support both sides of that debatable argument. Your job is to take the competing facts, consider both sides of the argument, and then take a position.

Let's use a self-defense example to show how to write an answer when the outcome is debatable. Before giving you the question, let me tell you an important self-defense rule that you will learn in your Criminal Law class: If a defendant kills someone and wants to claim self-defense, he must show that he reasonably believed that deadly force was necessary to protect himself from death or serious bodily harm. With that in mind, here is a very short essay question:

David and Victor met in the Army Special Forces thirty years ago when they were both 20 years old. Special Forces training is intense and often creates a bond between soldiers. David and Victor became close friends during training and have remained friendly ever since. David and Victor's Special Forces training included marksmanship (shooting), extensive physical fitness criteria, jumping from a plane, and learning how to navigate through a jungle. David and Victor both passed the Special Forces training with flying colors.

After training ended, David became a life-long military officer. In his spare time, David learned jujitsu by taking classes at a private dojo off the military base. By contrast, Victor was not interested in learning additional skills after Special Forces training. Indeed, Victor was not even interested in staying in the Army. Victor had a drinking problem, and he found the Army stifling. After being caught drunk multiple times, Victor was dishonorably discharged just a few years after he completed Special Forces Training.

Despite being dishonorably discharged, Victor did not find it hard to get a job in the private sector. Victor was 6'4" tall, and he was quite imposing when you stood near him. A fancy country club hired Victor to work as a security guard. Not much happened at the country club, and most days Victor just sat around and drank beer. Victor "worked" at the country club for nearly thirty years. Unfortunately, decades of drinking and lack of activity led to Victor having a heart attack a few years ago. Still, Victor kept drinking.

Last week, David confronted Victor about his excessive drinking. Victor (who had been drinking until five minutes

> before the confrontation) did not like to be challenged and he picked up a metal pipe, raised it over his head, and began to walk quickly toward David. When Victor was within 15 feet, David pulled out his gun and shot Victor. Victor died.
>
> The prosecutor has charged David with murder. You work for the defense attorney assigned to represent David. Write a memorandum explaining to your boss whether you think David will be able to assert a claim of self-defense.

Your first job on the exam will be to follow Tip #6 and state the governing rule of self-defense: As I told you above, the typical rule is that a person is permitted to use deadly force to defend himself if he reasonably believes an aggressor is going to kill him or inflict serious bodily injury. In other words, David was permitted to use deadly force if he reasonably thought that Victor was going to use the metal pipe to kill him or cause serious bodily harm.[1] The professor will likely give you some points for correctly stating the rule, but what she is really looking for is your analysis of whether David's actions were reasonable given the facts in the question.

The first thing to notice is that there is no clear right answer. David and Victor are described on paper. We don't know if one of them is more believable than the other. We can't get a feel for exactly how big Victor was and whether he was much larger than David. Nor do we have a good picture of what the scene looked like as the events unfolded. Was Victor stumbling drunk as he approached David with pipe? Or did Victor seem in control of his movements? These are questions for a jury to decide, and different juries might assess the witness's credibility differently. So your

---

[1] There are other issues to analyze as well, such as whether the threat David faced was sufficiently imminent. For simplicity purposes, let's leave the other issues aside.

professor is not looking for you to speculate about whether the jury would believe David to be a compelling witness.

Instead, your professor wants you to analyze the facts provided and make arguments about the strength of David's self-defense claim. This requires you to analyze both sides of the argument—the case for a valid self-defense claim, and the argument that a self-defense claim should fail. Here is an example of how you should write up the first part of that analysis:

> *There is some compelling evidence that David reasonably believed he faced death or serious bodily harm. First, Victor was very large (6'4" tall) and "quite imposing." Additionally, Victor was holding a metal pipe and he was holding it "over his head." A metal pipe is a dangerous weapon, particularly when it is raised over a person's head in such a position that the person could quickly strike. Moreover, Victor was not your average person. In addition to being very tall and imposing, he was trained in the Special Forces. Members of the Special Forces are probably better trained at using force than most people in society. Victor was also a heavy drinker. People who drink heavily often have impaired judgment and are probably more prone to lash out at others and be violent. The fact pattern tells us that Victor "did not like to be challenged" and that he immediately picked up the pipe upon being challenged. Piecing it all together, David faced a large, seemingly angry man, who he knew to be extremely well-trained in the use of force who was coming at him with a dangerous metal pipe raised over his head. Because of Victor's size, training, and use of a dangerous weapon, it was reasonable for David to believe he had to use deadly force (by shooting Victor) in order to protect himself from death or serious bodily injury.*

That answer sounds pretty good. Notice how much the answer engages with the facts in the question. It goes through each of the facts favoring David and pieces them into a narrative that supports a self-defense claim. Moreover, notice that the answer quotes important information from the question such as Victor being "quite imposing" and that the metal pipe was being held "over his head." In short, the answer is well-reasoned and tightly written. It seems right to me, and a lot of juries might agree with it.

If you only write the answer above, you will have done a passable job on the exam. I say passable because even though it is well-written and reasoned, the answer is definitely incomplete. The prosecution has a counter argument that deadly force was not necessary under the facts in the question. And you should not ignore the counterargument (even if you personally find it unpersuasive). Here is what the counterargument would look like—and imagine it coming right after the answer written above:

> *Of course, Victor posed a threat to David. He was wielding a dangerous weapon and coming directly at David. But it's important to remember the mismatch between the two people. First, Victor was likely drunk. Drunk people are less coordinated and more easily disarmed. Additionally, after years of alcohol ravaging his body, Victor had a heart attack that almost certainly left him much weaker than before his heart problems. Moreover, it has been roughly three decades since Victor was an Army Special Forces officer. So while Victor once had Special Forces training he has not been receiving continued training and he has likely forgotten some (or perhaps most) of what he learned decades ago. Victor is now about 50 years old and mostly sits around drunk all day. In short, Victor is likely pretty weak from a physical*

standpoint. He poses far less of a danger than he did when he was a young healthy adult.

Second, we must consider David's ability to disarm Victor. David is a "life-long military officer," which suggests that he remains on active duty in the Army. If he is in fact actively in the military (particularly if he is still in the Special Forces), David likely has to maintain a high level of physical fitness. Moreover, the question tells us that David studied jujitsu. Because of David's physical fitness and martial arts training, he was well situated to disarm Victor.

Indeed, when we combine David's strengths and Victor's weaknesses, it would be quite plausible for a jury to conclude that David was in a position to disarm Victor's metal pipe and defuse the situation without resort to deadly force. Because David was in a position to disarm Victor, a reasonable person in his position would not conclude he was in fear of death or serious bodily harm from Victor and his metal pipe.

The counterargument rejecting a self-defense claim is pretty solid. Nevertheless, I'm more persuaded that David has a valid self-defense claim. The reason is that it's hard to know whether someone in David's position would truly be able to disarm Victor, and the law tends to give the benefit of the doubt to the person being attacked. So, I would add a concluding paragraph that says something like the following:

Even though there are plausible arguments that David could have disarmed Victor, those arguments are speculative. Given the expansive law of self-defense, the better answer is that a reasonable person in David's shoes would believe deadly force is necessary to prevent death or serious bodily harm.

Personally, I think that's the right conclusion. But it's not the only plausible conclusion. The key point is that the answer is debatable. In other words, I cannot say for certain that the right answer is finding that David acted in self-defense. So if a student did all of the analysis above (i.e. explaining the argument for self-defense and also the argument against self-defense) I would not care which outcome they chose. I would accept either conclusion (as would every professor I know). The reason why is that professors care less about the outcome you pick than we do about the analysis you used to get to that outcome.

In short, when an issue is debatable, professors really don't care too much about which position you take. Rather, we care that you (1) considered both possible outcomes, (2) carefully applied the facts to the legal rules, and (3) actually took a position on what the outcome should be.

The third point—actually taking a position on the outcome—is important and worth focusing on because a lot of students miss it. So before we end this chapter, let me show you a much weaker answer that fails to take a position. I wrote the paragraph below myself, but I have seen similar paragraphs hundreds of times over the years. This is what you want to ***avoid*** doing:

> *The rule is that David can use self-defense if he reasonably believes he will be killed or suffer serious bodily harm. The defense would argue that Victor is very large (6'4"). The prosecution would argue that Victor had a heart attack and is probably not very strong. The defense would argue that Victor has a dangerous weapon over his head that he could use to strike David. The government would argue that David is trained in jujitsu and could easily disarm Victor. The defendant would argue that drunk people are dangerous and unpredictable. The government would argue that drunk*

people are slow and easy to disarm. The outcome could go either way.

There are two main problems with the answer above and they are connected. First, a laundry list of "the defense would argue," and "the government would say" is not really a cogent argument. It's just a list. Lawyers are in the business of stitching together coherent arguments, not laundry lists.

Second, and related, the answer above does not take a position. Even though your professor probably doesn't care whether you find that David acted in self-defense or not, she does want to see that you can piece together an argument. And the best way to piece together an argument is to stake out a position. Put differently, you do not need a lot of legal training to list some facts and say "the outcome could go either way."

Now that I've given you 10 positive tips for doing well on a law school exam, let me be negative for just a moment and tell you five quick things *not* to do on your exam answers.

- **Do Not Waste Time Writing Introductions or Conclusions to Your Answer.** As I've repeated over and over in this chapter, professors give out points for rules, applications of facts, and analysis. Professors almost never award points for writing a tidy summary or a beautiful introduction. It is repetitive to write a summary paragraph that repeats all the things you just wrote a few paragraphs earlier. Professors don't give out bonus points for repeating yourself. Nor do you need to write us an introduction that says, "Mens rea is an important concept" or "Offer and acceptance are crucial parts of any Contracts analysis." None of that stuff helps to analyze the issues, and professors therefore ignore it when they are grading. So don't spend time writing things that the professor won't give you points for.

- **Do Not Regurgitate the Facts Just to State Them.** The professor wrote the exam question and does not need large chunks of the question re-written back to them. Students sometimes re-state lots of facts at the beginning of their exam answer—likely because there are a million ideas spinning in their head and they don't know where to start. Repeating lots of facts as you start writing is probably not a bad brainstorming strategy when you are writing a paper for a seminar course. But it's not useful on a law school exam, which values precision and analysis. As discussed in Tip # 7, you should weave the important facts into your answer and use "because" to say why the facts matter to your conclusions. That is very different than just repeating the text of the question at the beginning of your answer without any analysis attached to those facts.

- **Do Not Give a Kitchen Sink Answer That Throws in Everything from Your Outline.** Sometimes when students have studied hard and know an issue well they want to show what they know, even if the question is not asking about that topic. Or sometimes students are not sure what the answer is and figure, "Well, if I write about everything, then something I say will be correct." Professors call this an "outline dump" or a "data dump." Please don't do this. It takes time to write each word, and you don't get credit for stating irrelevant rules. A law school exam is like surgery where you use a scalpel, not like a home renovation where you use a sledgehammer.

You should figure out the right rules and use them in the right spot. Be precise. Don't try to blast the exam with every ounce of ammunition in your arsenal.

- **Do Not Cut and Paste Text from One Part of Your Answer to Another.** Some issues come up repeatedly on an exam. It's a good bet you will write about mens rea multiple times in your Criminal Law exam and negligence multiple times in your Torts exam. After explaining one of those important doctrines, you may be tempted to cut and paste what you have already written and drop it into another part of your exam later on. Professors hate when you do that because it suggests to us that you think legal doctrine can be dropped in anywhere without regard to the factual differences between one scenario and another. If a professor has a negligence issue in one part of an exam and then another negligence issue later in the exam it's a pretty good bet that the facts or legal issues in the two situations are quite different. (Why would a professor test the same concept twice?) When you cut and paste the same text into multiple parts of your answer it suggests you don't get the nuances. So don't cut and paste.
- **Do Not Talk About the Exam After It's Over.** In every 1L class there are a couple of students who like to talk about the exam after it's over. Don't be that person. Here are three reasons why. First, almost no one likes to be around the person who fixates on the exam after it's over. If you are that person, be prepared for your friends to ditch you for the post-exam celebration at the bar. Second, your exam

answer will not get any better by discussing it afterwards. It is written and done. It's over. Third, and most important, fixating on what you got wrong on the last exam will put you in a bad head space for the next exam. Even if you wrote a great exam answer, there will be things you missed or messed up. If you figure out the issues you missed and the things you got wrong, that will gnaw at you. Remember that no one can spot all the issues and analyze everything perfectly when you are under time pressure. The dirty secret is that if your professors had to take their own exams, they would miss a few of the issues too. No one gets everything right. You don't need to be reminded of your mistakes on exam #1 before you take exam #2 a few days later. So don't talk about the exam after it's over. Walk away from that exam. Forever.

Points to Remember

- Do the reading and attend class all semester.
- Don't worry about being nervous for your exam. Everyone is nervous, even if they pretend they're not.
- Read the exam question twice before you write anything. Don't start typing your answer early just because other people do.
- Outline your answer with headings before diving into any one issue.
- Take the time to write clear sentences and paragraphs. But don't waste time trying to make your writing perfect.
- Remember to state the rule before jumping to your conclusion.
- Pull out the most important facts from the question and quote them back to the professor when they are important to an

issue. Use the word "because" as much as possible when explaining why the facts and the rule lead to a conclusion.

- Don't change clear facts in the question. You can suggest additional facts when they are missing and would contribute to the analysis.
- Focus on debatable issues, consider both sides, and take a position.
- Don't waste time writing introductory or conclusion paragraphs. And don't regurgitate the facts at the beginning of your answer unless you are connecting them to a specific issue.
- Don't give a kitchen sink answer that throws in everything from your outline. Write like you are a surgeon using a scalpel rather than doing a demolition with a sledgehammer.
- Don't cut and paste what you have written in one part of your answer into another part. Each section requires unique analysis.
- When the exam is over walk away and don't talk about it. You've worked hard, but it's time to move on.

CHAPTER 15

Extracurricular Activities

There is a ton of stuff to do in law school besides going to class. Most law schools have law journals that you can try out for, moot court programs that you can compete in, and a club for just about every imaginable legal interest. Let me offer three related pieces of advice about extracurricular activities:

1. It is important to join some clubs and organizations.
2. It is important not to join too many clubs and organizations.
3. Don't join a club or try out for a competition team or a journal just because everyone else is doing it or because you think you have to.

Let's start with rule 1. There are a couple of reasons why it is important to join some clubs and organizations. First, you are brand new to law school. It's good to meet people. And if you join student organizations that hold at least some interest for you, then you are likely to meet some like-minded students. Law school can be stressful. It's important to make friends.

Second, some student organizations do service projects and other cool stuff. And they often have interesting speakers come to campus to meet their members. If you aren't part of the group, you will likely miss some interesting events.

The first two reasons to join clubs were for your personal happiness. The next few reasons are more practical: Joining student organizations helps to improve your odds of getting a job. Before you know it, you will be looking for an externship or a job for the summer after your 1L year. There might be a few employers out there who *only* care about your grades. But I have never met them. And if they do exist, they're probably a little weird and not the kind of people you want to work for.

Every employer I've ever met wants to see that you have interests outside of class. So the third reason to join student organizations is to show employers that you're well-rounded. They want to see that you are capable of interacting with other people. They don't want to hire a genius who sits in the library all day but who has zero other interests. So you have to have something to put on your resume besides your grades. Joining a student organization also enables you to take a leadership position in that organization and to develop some important skills that will serve you well as a leader.

Fourth, and related, once you get interviews for summer jobs (and eventually interviews for permanent jobs) you are going to have to talk about something during those interviews. Like most law students, I did lots of interviews. Some went well. Others didn't. But all of them asked me questions about the student organizations listed on my resume.[1] Employers can read your transcript, so they don't really need to quiz you on legal concepts to figure out how

[1] Well, almost all of them. My one exception was a law firm partner who asked me questions about personal jurisdiction for the entire interview. I didn't much enjoy that interview and the feeling was apparently mutual because the law firm didn't offer me a job.

smart you are. If there's nothing on your resume besides your grades, there's a good chance the interview will be painful.

Fifth and finally, student organizations sometimes have contacts with alumni and employers. Being part of the organization can help you to meet future employers.

So it's obviously a good idea to join some student organizations. But it's also important not to join a ton of them. Your time is valuable and limited. Student organizations should be a break from studying, not a huge obligation. When you join an organization, you should probably attend some of its events. Indeed, the student organization may even pressure you to attend a bunch of events. That's fine, as long as you're not committed to too many groups. To say it again, your time is your most valuable commodity. Don't give it up recklessly. To help guide you, follow these 5 simple rules:

1. Don't skip your reading to attend extracurricular events.
2. Don't skip going to class.
3. Leave enough time to consolidate your class notes at the end of the week.
4. Leave time for outlining.
5. Make sure you're getting enough sleep.

If you can meet those 5 prerequisites, it's fine to spend your other time doing extracurricular activities. In other words, make sure you do your regular school work and take care of your well-being first. With those basic principles in mind, let's talk about the different types of student organizations.

Organizations Focused on a Type of Law: Many schools have student organizations based on subject area. For example, your school might have a Business Law Society, a Criminal Law Society, an Employment Law Society, an Immigration Law Society, or an International Law Society, to name just a few. These organizations often have interesting speakers, and they can be a good networking tool.

Organizations Focused on Personal Background: These are groups based around heritage, race, religion, sexual orientation, or other identities. For instance, many law schools have a Black Law Students Association, a Christian Law Society, and an organization focused on LGBTQ+ issues. These organizations and others like them are sometimes called affinity groups. These groups are a good opportunity to meet people with similar backgrounds, experiences, and interests.

Organizations That Send a Signal About Politics: Many law schools have chapters of the Federalist Society and the American Constitution Society. Students who are interested in constitutional law, the Supreme Court, and other "public law" topics may be very interested in the events sponsored by these organizations. Indeed, some of the most interesting (and sometimes controversial) speakers are sponsored by these groups. Being part of these organizations (particularly if you are later elected to a leadership position) provides a great opportunity to meet important people in the legal world. But you should be aware that these two organizations carry political connotations. The national Federalist Society is a powerhouse player in the conservative legal movement. The American Constitution Society typically addresses controversial issues with a more liberal bent. It's of course fine to join either (or both if you want to hear and meet the speakers they bring to campus!) But be aware that having either organization's name on your resume sends a message (whether intended or not) about your political beliefs. That may not be an issue for you, but it's best to be aware.

Moot Court and Mock Trial Competition Teams: Most schools have moot court and mock trial teams. Many schools also have other teams focused on negotiation, arbitration, business transactions, and other topics. To get on these teams you will do a try-out, usually during your 1L year. Then, as a 2L and 3L you will compete against teams from other law schools. Competition teams can be a great experience, but they can also be very time-consuming, so I'm going to give you some background on the different types of teams and some words of caution before you sink a lot of time into trying out.

Moot court is usually the most prominent of the competition teams. Let's talk about the experience once you're on the team. Students act as appellate lawyers, but without real cases. Students are assigned a detailed fact pattern and a transcript with the record of the "case." Students then write a brief and present oral argument before a panel of "judges." I put "judges" in quotes because often the judges are professors or alumni. (Sometimes in the final round the competitors argue before real judges.) Moot court is a great way to begin learning how to be an advocate. In some schools, the moot court program is a big deal. Winning a tournament as a 2L or 3L student is prestigious and can be a ticket to a fancy job. In other schools, the moot court program is just an extracurricular activity like any other.

Mock trial is, not surprisingly, a trial-based exercise. Students act as trial lawyers in simulated legal proceedings. They make opening statements, present witnesses and evidence, and make closing arguments. The experience is supposed to be like a real trial except that none of the parties are real, hence the word "mock."

The other competitions follow this same model. For instance, arbitration teams involve doing a mock arbitration (settling a dispute outside of the traditional court process). Transactional teams simulate corporate dealmaking and students are judged in the tournament by corporate lawyers and professors.

As noted above, moot court, mock trial, and the other teams are competitive to get onto. There are a fixed number of spots and they don't take everyone. So students have to try out in order to get a spot.[2]

Unfortunately, in many schools the tryouts for the moot court, mock trial, and other competition teams occur during the 1L year. Indeed, in some schools, the tryouts for some of the subject specific competition teams (e.g. the Alternative Dispute Resolution Team) may occur in the fall semester of your 1L year. That is crazy. Students who are only a few weeks into law school do not know enough yet to be doing tryout competitions. And, of course, students should be focused on their classes during their first semester. Alas, in some schools the student organizations have free reign to set their tryouts when they want. And they want to grab students early to make sure their team gets enough good people.

With tryouts happening during your 1L year, you have some decisions to make. You will likely feel some pressure to try out because lots of your classmates will be trying out. Additionally, you will feel like you have to try out because this is your "one chance" to make it onto a team and you don't want to miss your opportunity. Finally, you might have some self-doubt about making one of the teams, so you might feel like you should hedge your bets and try out for multiple (or, worse yet, all) of the competition teams to make sure you get on one. Before you know it, you may be writing briefs and preparing oral arguments for multiple competitions, instead of focusing on the reading for your actual classes. This is not a recipe for success.

So let me give you some simple advice about how to navigate the competition team situation. Do not try out for teams just

---

[2] By contrast, the student organizations that focus on legal interests and background (e.g. the Criminal Law Society or the Christian Law Society) usually take all interested students.

because it seems like everyone else is doing it. You've heard the old adage, "Would you jump off a bridge just because everyone else did?" Obviously not.

If you've made it this far in the book, I hope you have some trust in what I'm telling you. So let me give you my permission not to try out for the competition teams. Your life will not end if you aren't on a competition team. You can still get a job and have a great legal career. Sure, being on a team looks good on your resume. But there are lots of other student organizations you can get involved in. And being on a competition team is not worth it if it will take up so much time that it negatively affects your ability to study for your classes.

Of course, I am also not telling you that the competition teams are a waste of your time. Participating in moot court and the other teams can be a great experience. But that just reinforces the point about jumping off the bridge. If there's something in the water that interests you, jump off that bridge. But don't jump off the moot court bridge if you want to be a mergers and acquisitions lawyer. Do things that make sense for you. That might include moot court or it might not.

Finally, if you decide to try out for the competition teams, pick one or two. Don't try out for everything. You don't have time for that. If you only try out for one or two teams and you don't get selected, that is not the end of the world. There are other organizations you can join, including the law journals described below.

Law Journals: Almost every law school has a "law review" that publishes legal scholarship on a wide variety of topics. In the past, "being on law review" was the biggest accomplishment in law school. Only a fraction of students made law review, and those spots went only to the students with the highest grades. Today, being on the law review is still a big deal, but perhaps not as huge of a deal as in the past.

Many schools also have "specialty" journals that publish articles exclusively about a particular subject area. For instance, the law school where I teach has a specialty journal about environmental law. Over the last 50 years there has been an explosion in the creation of specialty journals. The school where I graduated from now has 9 specialty journals! While your law school may not have that many, it's a good bet that your school will have other journals besides *the* law review. That means that while there are still only a small number of spots on *the* law review, there are lots of opportunities to be on *a* law journal.

Let's talk about what the journals do, what your role would be, and what the tryout process is like. Law journals publish legal scholarship on every imaginable topic. Professors (and some lawyers) write lengthy articles with hundreds of footnotes. They then submit those articles to lots of journals. The managing board of the journals (students who are elected to senior positions) decide which articles to publish. The journals then do extensive editing and cite-checking of the articles before publishing them in legal databases.

Everyone who makes it onto a journal starts with the title of "editor." As noted above, the articles typically have hundreds of footnotes that reference other articles and books. The job of the journal editors is to find each of the sources cited in the footnotes and check them to makes sure the author is quoting or citing the sources accurately. Additionally, the editors check the formatting of the footnotes to make sure that the citations are in the correct format (called "blue booking"). In short, as an editor you will be finding sources, checking the accuracy of citations, and then fixing the way those citations are written to make sure they conform with the style manual. Almost everyone finds this work to be boring at best and excruciating at worst.

Additionally, as a journal editor you are usually obligated to write a student "Note." Notes are long scholarly papers—kind of like junior varsity versions of the articles that professors write. A more senior member of the law journal will work with you to help you pick a topic, outline your argument, and shape your writing. A small number of the Notes will be published in the law journal alongside the professors' articles. The Note writing process will make you a better writer, but it is a huge amount of work.

So how do you get this rather boring job where you do a lot of work and don't get paid for it?[3] At most schools, there is a tryout competition right after you finish your 1L year. The process differs from school to school, but usually you are given a packet of cases and articles and assigned a task such as writing a paper or a judicial opinion based on the sources provided. Additionally, most schools also have a citation test in which you are given citations and have to fix them using the Blue Book Style manual that you learned about in your Legal Writing course. On the plus side, most schools run a "joint" tryout process where you only do one tryout and you can submit it to multiple journals.

The managing boards of the journals then review the tryout submissions and in the case of *the* law review possibly factor in grades depending on the school's process. A few months after you do the tryout, you may then be offered a position as an editor on the journal.

At this point, you might be saying to yourself "Why on earth should I want to be a journal editor?" It's a lot of tedious work and an extra test that I have to take after my grueling final exams." The

[3] Some students have started a movement for law journal editors to get paid for their work. It has not gained much traction though.

main reason to try out for journals has historically been for resume value and helping yourself to get a job. Most legal employers have long thought two things about being on a journal, only one of which makes sense. First, employers think that it is prestigious to be on a journal. (This is the thing that makes no sense.) Second, employers think that the work of being on a journal teaches students to pay close attention to details and also teaches them to learn citation and editing skills that they may use in legal practice. (This rule at least makes some sense.)

So should you try out for a journal? The answer for most people is "yes." Being on a journal is a great line to put on your resume and it will help your writing and editing skills. While it can be boring and a lot of work, some difficult things are worth doing in life. There are caveats though. For instance, if you want to be a prosecutor, most district attorney's offices don't really care whether you are on a journal. The same may be true for a few other types of employers. Consult with your school's career services office.

Points to Remember

- Join some student organizations. They are a great way to make friends and to add something to your resume. But don't join more organizations than you have time for.
- Don't let student organizations get in the way of your studying. Your classes should come first.
- Moot court, mock trial and other competition teams can be a great experience, but don't try out just because everyone else is doing it.
- If you don't make a competition team, your life will go on. Don't feel compelled to try out for lots of teams just to ensure you make one of them.

- Most students should do the tryout competition to become a law journal editor. It can be tedious work, but it will help you with employment.

A Glossary of Terms for the 1L Year

General Terms

- **0L:** Someone who is about to start their first year of law school
- **1L:** First-year law student
- **2L:** Second-year law student
- **3L:** Third-year law student
- **Δ:** The symbol used to represent the defendant
- **π:** The symbol used to represent the plaintiff
- **ABA:** The abbreviation for the "American Bar Association."
- **Amicus Curiae:** A Latin phrase meaning "friend of the court." Often abbreviated to just "amicus" for singular and "amici" for plural. Amicus or Amici are people or organizations who, although they are not a party to a case, have an interest in the outcome. They submit a brief to the court with additional information or advocating a particular outcome.

- **Appeal:** When someone challenges a lower court's decision, they appeal by asking a higher court to review and change that decision.
- **Appellant:** The party that files an appeal.
- **Appellee:** The party that won in the court below and who will argue that the lower court's ruling was correct.
- **Bar Exam:** The test everyone dreads. Most states require you to take the bar exam in order to practice law.
- **Big Law:** The career path of working at a large, prestigious law firm, often representing large corporations in high-stakes litigation and deals.
- **Black Letter Law:** The longstanding doctrinal rules for a particular area of law. Your professor will often teach the "black letter rules" that are most common around the country, rather than the rules of any one particular state.
- **Bluebook:** A citation guide that shows you (in painful detail) the correct way to cite cases, court documents, treatises, and every other imaginable source.
- **Brief:** The short document you create for the cases in your assigned reading. Your brief will include the facts, the issue, the holding, and the reasoning of each case. You write a brief to help you understand the cases and perform well if you're called on in class. See Chapter 9 for advice on how to write a brief.
- **Burden of Proof:** The level of certainty that one party has to prove in order to win. For example, the burden of proof in criminal cases is "beyond a reasonable doubt." The burden of proof in a torts case is by a "preponderance of the evidence."
- **CALI:** The award at many law schools that goes to one student who earned the highest grade in a course.

- **Casebook:** This is your textbook for the class. It is filled with cases and questions. It doesn't list the legal rules. You'll use the cases and the discussion of them in class to figure out the rules.
- **Certiorari:** How the Supreme Court of the United States reviews decisions of lower courts. If certiorari is granted, the Court hears the case. If certiorari is denied, the lower court decision stands. It is often referred to as "cert."
- **Cir.:** The abbreviation for "Circuit."
- **Civ.:** The abbreviation for "Civil."
- **Civil Procedure:** This is the set of rules that governs how lawsuits are conducted in civil cases. It is also a class you will take as a 1L.
- **Clerkship:** A clerkship is a temporary position held by a recent law school graduate. Clerks work for a judge, mainly doing research and drafting opinions.
- **Cold Call:** When the professor randomly, and without notice, calls on you to answer questions.
- **Common Law:** Law that comes from judicial decisions instead of statutes. It is judge-made law that has evolved over centuries.
- **Competition Team:** Law schools often have multiple teams that law students can join, including Moot Court, Mock Trial, and Alternative Dispute Resolution. Students argue hypothetical cases in front of lawyers and judges.
- **Complaint:** The document that starts a lawsuit. The plaintiff files it as a way to explain the reasons why they are suing.
- **Concurrence:** An opinion from a judge when they agree with the decision of the majority of the court, but want to explain why they see the issue somewhat differently.

- **CREAC:** The abbreviation for the legal writing approach called "Conclusion, Rule, Explanation, Analysis, Conclusion." Similar to IRAC (see below) but in CREAC you start with the conclusion instead of the issue.
- **Defendant:** The person being sued or accused in a case.
- **Deposition:** This is a discovery procedure in which an individual or company has to answer questions under oath before trial.
- **Discovery:** The information-gathering part of a lawsuit. It occurs before trial, and both sides get to obtain evidence from the other party.
- **Dissent:** An opinion from a judge when they disagree with the decision of the majority of the court.
- **FRCP:** The abbreviation for the "Federal Rules of Civil Procedure."
- **Gunner:** The over-confident student who participates too much in class, often raising their hand when they suspect the student called on will not be able to answer. Other students often dislike the gunner.
- **Holding:** The key point the court is deciding. The holding of the case is the answer to the key legal question posed.
- **Hypo:** A hypothetical set of facts that professors use to expand your understanding of the material.
- **Id.:** An abbreviation meaning "the same." It is used in legal citations to signify that a previously cited source is being cited again.
- **IRAC:** The abbreviation for the legal writing approach called "Issue, Rule, Analysis, Conclusion." Similar to CREAC (see above) but with IRAC you start with the issue instead of the conclusion.

- **Judicial Internship:** A judicial internship is similar to a clerkship, but it is a temporary position held by a law student instead of a law school graduate. Judicial interns assist with research and drafting opinions, often over summers or during the academic year.
- **Jurisdiction:** The authority of a court to hear a case.
- **K:** A weird abbreviation for "contract" that your professor may use.
- **Law Review/Journal:** Student-run publications that publish articles and essays written by professors and students. Law schools typically have one "main" law review that publishes all types of scholarship, and one or more "specialty" journals that focus on a specific area of law.
- **Litigation:** The process of suing someone or taking legal action against a party. It includes the entire process of a lawsuit from start to finish.
- **LRW:** The abbreviation for "Legal Research and Writing."
- **Motion:** A formal request made to the court by a party asking the judge to do something or rule on a specific issue.
- **MPRE:** The Multistate Professional Responsibility Exam. The MPRE is a multiple-choice test on professional ethics, which you will have to pass before you can be admitted to the bar.
- **Opinion:** The court's written explanation of its decision in a particular case. Opinions include not just the outcome but also the reasoning behind a decision.
- **Oral Argument:** The presentation of a case by lawyers in front of a judge or multiple judges during which the lawyers argue their case and answer any questions the judge(s) may have.
- **Outline:** The document students create to prepare for exams. It sets out all the key rules you've learned over the semester.

- **Petitioner:** A person who files a request, or a petition, in a court.
- **Plaintiff:** The person who initiates a lawsuit, usually seeking damages of some sort.
- **Precedent:** A previous court decision that serves as a rule or guide for future cases.
- **Remand:** When an appellate court sends a case back to the lower court for further proceedings, essentially telling the lower court to try again.
- **Respondent:** The person responding to the petitioner. The respondent defends against the petitioner's claims.
- **Restatements:** Summaries of the law in a particular area written by legal scholars. They are persuasive to courts, but they are not binding.
- **SBA:** The abbreviation for the "Student Bar Association"—the name at many law schools for the student government.
- **SCOTUS:** The abbreviation for the "Supreme Court of the United States."
- **Socratic Method:** The teaching technique used by most 1L professors to run their classes. The professor calls on students and questions them about the case they read and hypothetical scenarios that are a little different than the cases. The professor uses the student's answers to elicit the legal rules.
- **Standard of Review:** The guidelines that appellate courts use to determine how much deference to give to a lower court's decision.
- **Stare Decisis:** The principle that courts should follow precedent.
- **Statute:** A written law passed by a legislative body.

- **Statute of Limitations:** The amount of time someone has to file a lawsuit after the injury or damage occurs. In criminal law, it is the amount of time the government has to file charges.
- **Study Guide/Aid/Supplement:** Books designed to help you understand an area of law and prepare for an exam. See Chapter 12 for an explanation of the different types of books and recommendations about what to buy and what not to buy.
- **Summary Judgment:** A decision made by the court in a civil case without a full trial. A court can issue summary judgment for one of the parties if there are not genuine factual issues in dispute and the court can decide solely based on the law.
- **Torts:** Civil wrongs that cause harm or loss and that lead to legal liability. Most frequently, torts deal with personal injuries and property damage.
- **Treatise:** A book that explains the law in great detail. Treatises are long and detailed, and they are definitely not for studying. You may use treatises to look up very detailed points of law.
- **U.C.C.:** The abbreviation for the "Uniform Commercial Code" a source of rules you will use for commercial transactions in your Contracts class.
- **Venue:** The location where a case is heard. Disputes over venue have to do with the most appropriate location based on the facts of the case.
- **Verdict:** The decision of a jury or judge in a trial.
- **Voir Dire:** The process of questioning potential jurors to determine whether they can be impartial on a jury.
- **Westlaw/Lexis Nexis/Bloomberg:** The legal research databases available to most law students.

Civil Procedure Terms

- **AICR:** The abbreviation for the "Amount in Controversy Requirement."
- **Discovery:** The part of a lawsuit where both sides share information and evidence before trial.
- **Diversity Jurisdiction:** When a federal court has subject matter jurisdiction to hear a case because the parties are from different states or countries and the amount in controversy is over $75,000.
- **Federal Question Jurisdiction:** When a federal court has subject matter jurisdiction to hear a case because it involves a question about federal law or the U.S. Constitution.
- **FRCP:** The abbreviation for the "Federal Rules of Civil Procedure."
- **Intervenor:** Someone who originally was not involved in the lawsuit but who joins a lawsuit on their own.
- **Motion to Dismiss:** When a party asks the court to throw out a case because there's a legal reason it shouldn't go forward. It could be because the complaint doesn't state a valid claim, or the court doesn't have jurisdiction.
- **Personal Jurisdiction:** Whether a court has power over the defendant.
- **Pleadings:** The official documents in a lawsuit. They include the complaint from the plaintiff stating the claims, and the answer from the defendant responding to those claims.
- **Subject Matter Jurisdiction:** Whether a court has the authority to hear the particular type of claim.

Constitutional Law Terms

- **Counter-Majoritarian Difficulty:** The challenge faced when unelected judges overturn laws passed by elected representatives, raising concerns about democratic legitimacy and the balance between majority rule and protecting minority rights.
- **DPC:** The abbreviation for the "Due Process Clause."
- **EPC:** The abbreviation for the "Equal Protection Clause."
- **Federalism:** The system where power is divided between the national government and the state governments, allowing both to make and enforce laws in their own areas. This balance helps prevent either level from becoming too powerful.
- **IC:** The abbreviation for "interstate commerce."
- **Intermediate Scrutiny:** The middle level of equal protection analysis to evaluate laws that affect certain protected classes (usually gender). The law must serve an important government interest and be substantially related to achieving that interest.
- **Originalism:** A method of interpreting the Constitution based on the intent or original understanding of the framers and the people at the time it was ratified.
- **Procedural Due Process:** The legal requirement that you must get a fair process (such as notice and a hearing) before the government can take away your life, liberty, or property. It ensures you have a chance to defend yourself.
- **Rational Basis Scrutiny:** The lowest standard of equal protection analysis. The law must be reasonably related to a legitimate government interest. Under this standard, courts usually uphold the law unless it's clearly arbitrary or irrational.
- **SCOTUS:** The abbreviation for the "Supreme Court of the United States."

- **Strict Scrutiny:** The highest standard of equal protection analysis, which is used to evaluate laws that affect fundamental rights or involve suspect classifications (like race). The law must serve a compelling government interest and be narrowly tailored to achieve that interest.
- **Substantive Due Process:** The principle that protects certain fundamental rights from government interference, even if the procedural steps for limiting the rights would be fair.
- **Textualism:** A method of interpreting the Constitution based on the plain meaning of its words, without considering external factors.

Contracts Terms

- **Acceptance:** When the other party agrees to the offer.
- **Breach:** When someone doesn't do what they promised in the contract.
- **Consideration:** What each party gives up in order to get what they want from the other party in the contract.
- **K:** The abbreviation for "contract."
- **O&A:** The abbreviation for "offer and acceptance."
- **Offer:** When one party proposes a deal to another.
- **Parol Evidence Rule:** The legal concept that once there is a written contract the parties cannot claim that previous oral or written statements not written in the contract are part of the deal.
- **PER:** The abbreviation for "parol evidence rule."
- **UCC:** The abbreviation for "Uniform Commercial Code."

Criminal Law Terms

- **Actus Reus:** The action that a defendant takes to commit a crime. For example, in theft cases, the actus reus is the grabbing of the property.
- **ALI:** The abbreviation for the "American Law Institute."
- **Burden of Proof:** The obligation to prove one's assertion. In criminal law, the prosecutor has the burden to prove each element of the crime beyond a reasonable doubt.
- **CL:** The abbreviation for the "common law."
- **Defenses:** The defendant's reason why they should not be found guilty of the crime, even if all the elements of the criminal offense have been demonstrated.
- **Mens Rea:** The defendant's mental state while committing the crime. The main mental states are purposely, knowingly, recklessly, and negligently.
    - Purposely: A defendant hopes something will happen.
    - Knowingly: A defendant is aware that something will almost certainly happen, even if they do not desire for it to happen.
    - Recklessly: A defendant is aware of a substantial and unjustifiable risk that their actions will cause harm, but they take the action anyway.
    - Negligently: A defendant is not aware of an unacceptable risk but they should have been aware of it.
- **MPC:** The abbreviation for the "Model Penal Code."

- **Strict Liability Offense:** A crime in which the prosecutor does not have to prove a mens rea. The prosecution only has to demonstrate that the defendant committed the actus reus.
- **U.S.C.:** The abbreviation for the "United States Code."

Legal Research and Writing Terms

- **Bluebook:** A uniform system of citation used in legal writing to ensure consistent and precise citation of legal authorities.
- **Citation:** A reference to a legal authority, such as a case, statute, regulation, treatise, or other source.
- **Dicta:** Statements made by a judge in a decision that are not essential to the ruling and do not have the force of law, but may be persuasive in future cases.
- **Headnote:** A brief summary of a particular point of law decided in a case, placed at the beginning of a case report.
- **Legal Memorandum:** An objective, internal document that analyze issues in a case and predicts how a court might rule on a legal issue. It presents the facts, issues, analysis, and conclusion.
- **Mandatory Authority:** Legal sources that a court must follow when deciding a case. For example, a lower court must follow the decisions of the appellate court in its jurisdiction, and all courts must adhere to the rulings of the U.S. Supreme Court on federal issues. Mandatory authority is binding on the court, meaning the court is required to apply it to the case at hand.
- **Persuasive Authority:** Legal principles and precedents from other jurisdictions or secondary sources that a court may consider but is not obligated to follow.
- **Primary Authority:** Legal sources that establish the law, such as statutes, regulations, and case law. These are binding on the courts within the relevant jurisdiction.

- **Secondary Authority:** Sources that explain, interpret, or analyze the law, such as law review articles and treatises. These are not binding but can be highly persuasive.
- **Shepardizing:** The process of checking a legal citation to see if it is still good law. This involves using Shepard's Citations to find the history and treatment of a case.
- **Westlaw/LexisNexis/Bloomberg:** Online legal research databases that provide access to case law, statutes, legal periodicals, and other resources.

Property Terms

- **Adverse Possession:** The legal principle by which a person comes to own a piece of property by openly occupying it for a certain period of time without the owner's permission.
- **Bona Fide Purchaser (BFP):** Someone who buys property in good faith, without knowing about any existing claims or issues, and pays a fair price.
- **Chattel:** Personal property that is movable, such as cars and cell phones. It's different from real property, which includes land and buildings.
- **Covenant:** This is a promise written into deeds or leases to do (or not do) something with the property.
- **Deed:** This is a legal document that transfers ownership of real estate from one person (or company) to another.
- **Easement:** This is a right to use someone else's property for a specific purpose. Common examples include the right to walk across someone's property to get to a public beach or a utility company's right to run power lines through a property.
- **Eminent Domain:** This is the government's power to take private property for public use, provided they pay just compensation.

- **Joint Tenancy (JT):** This is a form of property ownership where two or more people own a property together, with equal rights. One key feature is the right of survivorship, meaning if one owner dies, the property automatically passes to the surviving owners.
- **Life Estate (L/E):** This type of ownership lasts for the duration of someone's life. Once that person passes away, the property either goes back to the original owner or to another designated person.
- **Tenancy by the Entirety (TBE):** This is a special form of joint property ownership for married couples where both co-own the property. Neither can sell their share without the other's consent, and if one dies, the other automatically owns the whole property.
- **Tenancy in Common (TC):** Property ownership without a right of survivorship. Each owner can sell or leave their share of the property to whoever they choose.
- **Title:** This is the legal term for ownership of property.
- **Zoning:** These are laws and regulations that govern how land can be used in different areas. Zoning laws dictate whether an area can be used for residential, commercial, or industrial purposes.

Torts Terms

- **Compensatory Damages:** Money awarded to cover the actual losses from an injury. Compensatory damages are awarded to make the victim "whole" for the harm they suffered.
- **Duty of Care:** A negligence concept in which people have a legal obligation to act reasonably to avoid causing harm.
- **Eggshell Plaintiff:** A rule that says a defendant is responsible for all damages caused, even if the plaintiff had preexisting

conditions that made the harm worse. You take the plaintiff as you find them.

- **Factual Causation:** Also known as "but-for" causation. This concept looks at whether the harm would have occurred "but for" the defendant's actions.
- **Hand Formula:** A formula to determine whether someone breached their duty of care. It is expressed as $B < P \times L$, which stands for Burden is Less Than Probability multiplied by Loss. If the cost of preventing the harm is less than the risk and potential damage combined the person acted negligently.
- **IIED:** The abbreviation for "intentional infliction of emotional distress."
- **Proximate Causation:** A concept that considers whether the harm was a foreseeable result of the defendant's actions. When the harm was not foreseeable the defendant will not be held liable.
- **Punitive Damages:** Money awarded to punish the wrongdoer and deter future bad behavior.
- **Reasonableness Standard:** A standard that measures how an average person would act in the same situation.
- **Strict Liability:** A doctrine that allows someone to be held responsible for any harm they caused, even if they did not act negligently or with another mens rea. It's often used for dangerous activities or defective products.